ODD LIFE. Good God.

A STUDY IN 1 PETER FOR
INDIVIDUALS, GROUPS, AND FAMILIES

REALFAITH.COM

Mark Driscoll

Odd Life. Good God. A Study in 1 Peter for Individuals, Families, &
Groups.

ISBN: 978-1-7351028-0-1 (Paperback)
ISBN: 978-1-7351028-1-8 (E-book)

All emphases in Scripture quotations have been added by the author.

CONTENTS

INTRODUCTION

The first version of this resource for personal Bible study, small groups, and families was originally published in 2009. It was the result of a group effort from myself, a research team, and some other team members. This is a completely rewritten and updated version of that resource. I pray it helps you, and those you love, learn from the leader of the disciples who spent three years learning directly from Jesus Christ. You can find the nine sermons preached in 2020 that correspond with this nine-part study guide, along with daily devotions that serve as a basic Bible commentary all for free, at **realfaith.com**. There, you will also find hundreds of other free sermons and thousands of free Bible teaching resources made possible by the generosity of our financial partners who support Real Faith as a Bible teaching ministry of Mark Driscoll Ministries.

Mark Driscoll

CHAPTER 1

PETER'S ODD LIFE AND GOOD GOD

"...behold, Satan demanded to have you, that he might sift you like wheat, but I have prayed for you that your faith may not fail. And when you have turned again, strengthen your brothers."

- Jesus and Peter's conversation in Luke 22:31-32

Sometimes, it can be hard to identify with the characters in the Bible because they seem so flawless and perfect. That is not the case with Peter. The one believer in the Bible that is perhaps the most imperfect is Peter.

Peter lived an odd life, which makes him likely the easiest person to identify with in the Bible. Perhaps no one in all of Scripture is as unpredictable and volatile, impulsive and hyper-responsive as Peter the Odd (Matthew 14:28; Mark 14:29; Luke 5:8; John 21:7). His decision-making is, at times, reminiscent of a junior high kid who has not slept in a few days filled with espresso. If Peter were alive today, it would be guaranteed that cameras would follow him around filming his every word and deed as yet another hit reality television show.

If Peter were playing an instrument in a high school band, he would be the guy always hitting the wrong note at the worst time. If Peter were in the military, he'd be the one person guaranteed to end up marching out of formation. If Peter were on a sports team, he'd trip over his own feet at the most inopportune time.

Peter's life is a roller coaster. On his worst days, he bossed Jesus around and denied even knowing Him. On his best days, he wrote two books of the Bible and, according to church history, was martyred by crucifixion for refusing to deny Christ. Peter asked his killers to turn his cross upside down because he did not believe he was worthy of dying as Jesus did. It's an odd life when you go from denying Christ publicly to dying for Christ publicly.

Like most of us, Peter rarely got it right the first time, or even the second time. Once he does get it right, he's prone to eventually get it wrong again. After failing miserably by denying Jesus Christ as a coward in the gospels, you'd think he'd have learned his lesson after seeing Jesus rise from death, appoint him as the head of a new global movement, and standing there likely with the same look as a basset hound that was just given the keys for a car to drive watching Jesus return to Heaven. Nope. By the book of Galatians, he's a coward again, and to make matters worse, has also picked up racism additionally.

Despite the fact that Peter would not likely make it through Bible college today without getting kicked out, his shadow looms over much of the New Testament. In the four lists of the twelve apostles (Matthew 10:2–4; Mark 3:16–19; Luke 6:13–16; Acts 1:13), Peter is always mentioned first because he is their recognized leader after Jesus. As their leader, Peter also acts as spokesman for the Twelve when the need arises (Matthew 15:15; 18:21; Mark 1:36–37; 8:29; 9:5; 10:28; 11:21; 14:29; Luke 5:5; 12:41).

In Peter, we see a run-of-the-mill, shockingly normal Christian disciple. Someone who really loves Jesus. Someone who really sins. Someone with whom God is really patient as they grow and mature, taking two steps forward then one step back, never near perfect but heading North as a general rule. Religious folks are a bit shocked that Jesus picked Peter as the leader of early Christianity. But, for the rest of us who know we are a mess for our Messiah, Peter is the kind of leader we can relate to. Peter is a Christian like the rest of us. Peter's imperfections are endearing, and his progress is encouraging. In the life of Peter, we learn that even though life is odd, God is good. God does perfect work through imperfect people.

If there's hope for Peter, there's hope for anyone. If there's hope for Peter, there's hope for you. Peter was odd, but God was good. That's the secret to Peter's success. Like a loving wise dad with infinite patience, God's grace grew and changed Peter, making him more like Jesus and less like the Hebrew version of Napoleon Dynamite, which is where he started. The secret to Peter's greatness was God's goodness.

PETER'S FAMILY

One of the best ways to get to know someone is to find out about their family and hometown. This same principle is true of getting to know people in the Bible. Peter is a real person who really lived roughly 2,000 years ago. Archaeologists are confident that they have excavated his home, and I travelled there some years ago with my wife Grace and our five children, who were young at the time. There, we learned a bit about his family and hometown.

Harper's Bible Dictionary says, "Originally named Simon, Peter was a Galilean fisherman (Mark 1:16; Luke 5:2; John 21:3), the son of John (Matthew 16:17; John 1:42; 21:15–17) and brother of Andrew. According to a tradition detailed in John 1:35–43, the brothers came from the village of Bethsaida (John 1:43; 12:21) and had been disciples of John the Baptist before they became disciples of Jesus. Peter was married (Mark 1:29–31; 1 Cor. 9:5). He is said to have owned a house in Capernaum (Mark 1:29)."[1]

Like ordinary folks, Peter had a hometown, worked a job, grew up in a family with parents and siblings, got married, and spent his life living and working not far from where he was born. Everything in his life was normal, until He met Jesus, and then everything changed. The same is true of each of us.

PETER'S NAMES

One of the things we do for people we love is give them a nickname. In our family, the person with the most nicknames is our beloved youngest son. On one funny occasion, someone who was with us for the first time stopped and asked, "What is the youngest son's actual name?" They had heard so many fond names and nicknames for the boy, but they had no idea what his actual name was.

Some people have had the same experience studying the life of Peter. Widely loved like an entertaining brother, he has a lot of names and nicknames. A guide to Christian history provides helpful technical information about the story behind Peter's name: "There are actually four forms of Peter's name in the New Testament: the Hebrew translated into Greek, 'Simeon' to 'Simon', and the Aramaic translated into Greek, 'Cephas' to 'Petros' (meaning "rock"). His given name was Simeon bar-Jonah (Matthew 16:17; cf. John 1:42), 'Simon the son of John.'...It is most likely that 'Simon' was not merely the Greek equivalent of 'Simeon' but that, having his home in bilingual Galilee,

'Simon' was the alternate form he used in dealings with Gentiles. In fact, it was quite common for a cosmopolitan Jew to employ three forms of his name depending on the occasion: Aramaic, Latin, and Greek. The double name 'Simon Peter' (or 'Simon called Peter') demonstrates that the second name was a later addition, similar to 'Jesus, the Christ.' The number of times that the Aramaic equivalent 'Cephas' is used (once in John, four times each in Galatians and 1 Corinthians), as well as its translation into the Greek (not common with proper names), indicates the importance of the secondary name. Both Aramaic and Greek forms mean 'the rock,' an obvious indication of Peter's stature in the early church (see below on Matt. 16:18). It is obvious that he was called 'Simon' throughout Jesus' ministry but came to be known as 'Peter' more and more in the apostolic age."[2]

As you learn more about the life of Peter from the Bible, this insight will be helpful. In other Bible books, such as the early church history book of Acts, Peter is reported using multiple names, so paying attention is helpful to your learning about this towering figure in Christian history.

PETER AND JESUS

Like most relationships, the way we make a new friend is often by an old friend introducing us to someone they know but we do not. The same is true of what Christians call evangelism. In its simplest form, evangelism is someone who is friends with Jesus introducing a friend to Jesus so that they can be a friend group together with Jesus.

Peter was first introduced to Jesus by his brother Andrew (John 1:41). Not long after, Jesus personally called Peter to trade fishing for fish for fishing for souls with the simple words in Mark 1:17, "Follow me, and I will make you become fishers of men." Later, Peter was again called by Jesus to join the special group of His twelve disciples (Mark 3:16). In that day, if you wanted to learn something, you would often have a teacher rather than a school. A teacher, or rabbi, would select only a few disciples to be their students. The disciple would often have a close personal relationship with their teacher, travelling with them, eating with them, and observing them. In this way, education was far more of an intimate mentoring relationship than taking classes and tests as is common today.

As if being chosen by Jesus was not enough, in addition to being added to the twelve, Peter was also picked by Jesus to be among His nearest and dearest friends. If you had to pick a few friends to spend the most time with, who would it be? Peter was one of the three disciples, along with James and John, who formed an inner circle or friend group around Jesus (Mark 5:37; 9:2; 14:33; cf. 13:3). As Jesus' closest relationships, this privileged access allowed Peter to be present with Jesus as much as anyone during His earthly ministry, including being an eyewitness to milestone events in world history. One example is the day that Peter saw the transfiguration of Jesus, something only a few people got to experience (Mark 9:2-13). Peter's firsthand life experience, in the closest community of any human beings with Jesus, was so significant that Peter refers back to it as proof of the validity and authority of his teaching about Jesus (1 Peter 5:1; 2 Peter 1:16).

JESUS' CONTROVERSIAL WORDS TO PETER ABOUT A ROCK

For high-profile leaders, there is likely at least one public controversy that follows them for their entire life. For Peter, his high-profile controversy regarding his commission from Jesus has followed him to this very day and has resulted in the family feud between Catholic Christians and Protestant Christians.

Matthew 16:16–19 records Jesus' commission of Peter:

> Simon Peter replied [to Jesus], "You are the Christ, the Son of the living God." And Jesus answered him, "Blessed are you, Simon Bar-Jonah! For flesh and blood has not revealed this to you, but my Father who is in heaven. And I tell you, you are Peter, and on this rock I will build my church, and the gates of hell shall not prevail against it. I will give you the keys of the kingdom of heaven, and whatever you bind on earth shall be bound in heaven, and whatever you loose on earth shall be loosed in heaven."

This section is one of the most debated passages of the entire New Testament, and in many ways a dividing line between Protestant and Catholic Christians. This old family feud has two main interpretations, with many variations. Raised Catholic, attending a Catholic school for a few years, and serving as an altar boy assisting the priest with mass, I was taught that this verse was the establishing of Peter as the first bishop of the church, leading to apostolic succession and the papacy where men, starting with Peter, had the power to forgive sins, and exercise the authority of heaven on earth. Once I started attending a Protestant church in college, I was told that the church was not founded on any man but Jesus Christ, including Peter, and the rock of our salvation is faith that confesses Jesus as the Christ and Son of God, as Peter did.

One Bible commentator summarizes the debate surrounding who or what the rock is, saying, "Maybe excessive heat has dimmed light on this matter. Peter is the spokesman of the Twelve, for good or ill. Nowhere is it clearer than here. At one moment he is commended as the recipient of divine revelation (17): the next sees him rebuked as the dupe of Satan (23). The Catholics have the more natural interpretation of the passage, up to a point. It is more probable that Peter (Petros in Greek) is the rock (petra in Greek) on which the church is to be built than that anything else, such as his faith, is given that role. The word-play is irresistible. The rock is not just Peter, however, but Peter in his confessional capacity. Peter, full of trust in the Son of God, is the one who will become the rock-man for the early church. He did become just that, as the early chapters of Acts reveal. It is Peter who preaches the first evangelistic sermon, but Peter as representative of the Twelve. And if the Catholics are right in thinking it is primarily Peter, albeit the believing Peter, who becomes the church's rock-man, the Protestants are surely right in pointing out that the passage contains no hint that this role should devolve on any successors in Rome or anywhere else. It affords no grounds for the claims preferred by the papacy; in fact, this verse was not attached to those claims until long after they were first put forward. The point is this: Jesus had found in Peter a real believer, and on that foundation he could build his church."[3]

Delving into the Greek language in which the New Testament was first written, a scholarly New Testament reference library resource adds further insight saying, "the name Peter means 'rock.' In the Greek text this word is masculine (spelled petros), and describes a small piece of rock (something like a pebble). The word used in the phrase on this rock is feminine (spelled petra) and describes a large boulder or a mass of rock such as that found at the cliffs along the seacoast. Although some have proposed that Peter was to become the rock on which the church would be built, it appears that Jesus was using a play on words that, in effect, made the very opposite point. We might paraphrase Jesus' words as follows: "You're a small rock, Peter, but upon the greater rock that you have confessed, the truth of who I am, I will build my church."[4]

The conclusion that Jesus Christ is the Rock upon which the church is founded is common in Scripture. In the book of Psalms alone, God is referred to as our rock at least 16 times, including Psalm 18:2, "The Lord is my rock and my fortress and my deliverer, my God, my rock..." Psalm 18:31 adds, "who is God, but the Lord? And who is a rock, except our God?"

Isaiah also repeatedly refers to God as our rock, including Isaiah 30:29 which speaks of, "the Lord" as "the Rock of Israel." The theme of God as our rock continues in the New Testament as 1 Corinthians 10:4 speaks of the rock that provided for God's people in the Old Testament saying "the Rock was Christ." Peter himself says that Jesus Christ is the rock in 1 Peter 2:8 calling Him "A stone of stumbling, and a rock of offense."

Jesus also told a parable that to build anything you want to last (like a global movement called Christianity), it is best to found it on the strong foundation of a "rock" (Luke 6:48). Ephesians 2:20 says the first rock, or cornerstone of Christianity, is Jesus Christ, "built on the foundation of the apostles and prophets, Christ Jesus himself being the cornerstone..."

The conclusion that the rock of the church is the confession that Jesus Christ is the rock also finds support in the early church. The New Bible Dictionary says, "either Peter's faith or the confession of Peter's faith that Jesus is the Christ is in fact the 'rock' is a very early Christian interpretation. For example, the early church father Origen says, "Rock means every disciple of Christ."[5]

It deserves noting that even if someone believes that the rock on which the church is founded is somehow Peter instead of Jesus, that view does not endorse or even infer the subsequent teaching of the Roman Catholic Church. To move on from Jesus' statement to an entire hierarchy and tradition that the Roman bishops are the successors of Peter, and that in every generation the Catholic Church through the succession of popes who have Peter's same basic spiritual authority, essentially hold the keys to the kingdom of God with uniquely divine authority on earth, is a bit like trying to jump a skateboard over the Grand Canyon. It's an incredible leap.

PETER IN THE EARLY CHURCH

My wife and I have the great blessing of godly older spiritual authority that knows us, loves us, and oversees us like mature spiritual fathers and mothers. One of these men had been faithfully serving his church for decades when the time of transition came. Wanting to learn as much as I could from the succession, I jumped on a plane to spend a few days with our pastor and his successor. The handoff was as smooth as an Olympic track relay team, and I am happy to report that the church is flourishing with a new senior leader.

Passing the baton from one leader to the next is hard enough, but handing it from Jesus Christ to anyone else has to stand as the most precarious leadership handoff in history. After His resurrection and before His ascension, the Lord Jesus needed to decide who He would hand the baton to. After defeating death, Jesus appeared in person to meet with Peter (Luke 24:34; 1 Corinthians 15:5). Following Peter's denial of Jesus, the gospel of John also closes with the epic face-to-face, reconciliation, "do you love me?" conversation between Jesus and Peter where he is commissioned to lead and feed the people of God. Peter had dropped the baton before Jesus died and needed to pick it up again. In this we see that ministry leaders are not perfect, but that God in His grace uses their imperfections to help them qualify for even greater ministry by learning through erring.

Church history picks up the story of the disciples after Jesus returned to Heaven in the book of Acts, which might be better titled the Acts of the Holy Spirit as He is the moving force pushing the message and ministry of Jesus to the nations. Acts opens with Peter clearly stepping forward as the leader of early Christianity to preach the legend-making and legacy-changing sermon on Pentecost (Acts 1:15). Seemingly no one questioned or opposed his leadership because He was appointed by Jesus and anointed by the Spirit.

God the Holy Spirit then fell from Heaven on the people in conjunction with Peter's preaching, as Jesus' prayer that the Kingdom would come was being fulfilled (Acts 2). Once the Spirit of God baptized the early church, just like Jesus after His baptism, the people of God were empowered to continue Jesus' ministry under the leadership of His hand-selected successor, Peter. From that moment onward, Peter is the preacher, leader, and public figure of the Church without question or opposition (2:14; 3:12). Peter is the one who represents Christ and Christianity to the Jewish leaders (4:8) and serves as the public authority for things such as the discipline of a married couple that died for lying to the Holy Spirit (5:3). God the Holy Spirit worked mightily through the early church, but the person who is most noted for having the hand of God rest upon them in power is none other than Peter (5:15).

As the gospel of Jesus Christ moved out of the Jewish nation to the nations of the earth, just as God had promised to Abraham, it is Peter who is prominent in leading mission work to new regions like Samaria and beyond (8:14). Over and over, the Spirit of God anoints Peter with power and appoints Peter for leadership. The moral of the story is more than your personality, past, or problems; it's the presence and power of God that makes a great leader. The lack of jockeying for position and power after Jesus ascended is rather shocking. There has never been a bigger leadership vacuum in human history, yet there was a supernatural degree of unity and submission to authority that the church has, sadly, struggled to maintain ever since. Peter was not perfect, but he filled the leadership vacuum left by Jesus' ascension and every Christian in world history has benefitted from him.

Significantly, the Jewish Peter from Israel is chosen by God to be a pioneer in expanding the Church of Jesus Christ beyond that nation of Israel and culture of the Jews to every nation and culture. This calling happened supernaturally, as God gave Peter a vision of his future ministry to Gentiles (10:1; 15:7). Once again, we see a supernatural element to Peter's life and ministry, the only way to make sense of such an ordinary person doing such extraordinary ministry. Stepping into his calling to bring Jesus to the nations immediately brings criticism upon Peter as religious people fail to share God's heart for the nations and care only for people like themselves (11:2). Like so many of us, the religious spirit of folks thinks that we are the good people who deserve God's love, and that God could not possibly love people we find annoying, offensive, or too sinful for salvation. Sadly, Peter takes a step back to his old wishy-washy ways (Galatians 2:11-14).

In Galatia, a church grew with a mix of self-righteous religious Jewish folks, and brand-new Christians who came from pagan backgrounds. In addition to loving Jesus, the religious folks wanted to impose a long list of requirements (e.g. circumcision for males) upon the new Christians to be considered full members of God's family and worthy of sitting down to eat a communion meal together with the entire church. The religious folks started the usual negative public relations attack on Peter, and sadly he caved in to pressure as a coward once again, just as he had when Jesus was crucified. Rather than holding his ground and preaching the grace of God, Peter let the rule-making, law-keeping, barking religious dogs run him off in fear.

As was his tendency, Peter did eventually come to repentance, owned his error, and fought the war against the religious folks so that people could become a Christian without also becoming Jewish. This opened the door for the gospel of Jesus Christ to get out to the nations, something Peter was the first to argue for at the Council which decided that Gentiles needed only Jesus and were not obligated to adopt any Jewish traditions (Acts 15:7). Had this battle not been won, the gospel would have lost. If we add anything to faith in Jesus Christ for salvation, we lose the gospel. In the same way, adding pollution to a pure glass of water makes it all impure.

Peter's failure stories remind us of the trap of the fear of man (Proverbs 29:25). Peter seemed to struggle with this a lot, as we all do. When faced with doing what was right, he would step forward. But as soon as the criticisms and attacks rolled in, he would step backward. Then, God would again push his timid son forward, which is an encouragement for us all.

As the Apostle Paul and others become more prominent in the early church history of Acts, the work of Peter gets harder to trace. The focus of church history moves into the new areas that churches were getting planted and the gospel was spreading. Therefore, it is difficult to determine exact details about exactly where Peter was and what he was doing in his latter days. Exceptions include a few details like his escape from prison (Acts 12:17), trip to Antioch (Galatians 2:11), and possible brief trip to Corinth (1 Corinthians 1:12). Timing the end of Peter's life, however, helps us establish the time by which he would have had to complete his writing of 1-2 Peter. Concerning the death of Peter, Bible commentator Karen Jobes writes: "There is virtual unanimity that the apostle Peter died in Rome in the mid-60s during the reign of Emperor Nero."[6]

PETER THE AUTHOR

For the average Bible reader, the authorship of 1 Peter seems easy enough. The letter opens saying it's from "Peter, an apostle of Jesus Christ".

However, some critics have said that it was impossible that Peter actually wrote 1-2 Peter and that this error of authorship undermines the credibility of these books of the Bible. We will now discuss then debunk each of their common criticisms.

One, critics say that Peter could not have written these letters because he was a common fisherman long ago. This is not only wrong, but also proud for many reasons. Just because someone lived a long time ago does not mean that they were dumb and we are smart. If anything, it seems like today we have an epidemic increase in foolishness, often starting on college campuses where people get degrees but not wisdom. Furthermore, just because you fish does not mean that you are a bumbling backwoods dolt. Ernest Hemingway is perhaps the most famous fisherman of all time, for example.

The fishing business that Peter helped run prior to ministry also seems to be a large company with many employees, boats, and perhaps a significant revenue stream. Boats were incredibly expensive, yet his company had many. If he was a wealthy businessman working in a diverse area with multiple languages it is entirely possible that he was like most successful business owners and rather smart and competent.

Two, critics of Peter writing the letter bearing his name are prone to argue that he could not have written the letter based on Acts 4:13, which says that Peter was not formally educated. However, this charge is not credible for five reasons.

1. The New Bible Commentary explains that Peter's critics in Acts 4:13 attack him for being uneducated, or unschooled, which then bolsters their point that 1-2 Peter were written by someone beyond Peter's education level thereby disproving his authorship. It

goes on to explain that since Peter quotes from the Greek translation of the Old Testament (Septuagint or LXX) rather than the original Hebrew, it could not possibly be Peter writing because that would require someone well versed in multiple languages, something beyond an uneducated fisherman. The commentary goes on to explain, "The style is, however, not so 'educated' as some would like to make out and in places it is much more the language of ordinary people. There is evidence that in Peter's time Greek, as well as Aramaic, was spoken in Galilee, and as a fisherman living in Capernaum on one of the great trade routes he would have had to speak Greek regularly. The fact that his own brother's name, Andrew, is a Greek one suggests that from boyhood Peter would have grown up with this language. Some thirty years' work of evangelism and teaching in a church which contained an increasing proportion of Gentiles would have made him more fluent in Greek..."[7]

Growing up and conducting business in an area where people from numerous cultures and languages converged, it would not be surprising that Peter was fluent in multiple languages. In the same way, we live and minister in Arizona which explains why our daughter is fluent and formally educated in English and Spanish, able to minister easily in both languages. She's also picked up Portuguese as she has a knack for languages and love for people. This kind of thing is not without precedent and quite common in places where multiple cultures converge.

2. The entire charge that Peter was uneducated hangs precariously on one verse of Scripture. It is helpful to note that the charge there is made by critics. Acts 4:13 says, "when they saw the boldness of Peter and John, and perceived that they were uneducated, common men, they were astonished. And they recognized that they had been with Jesus."

   For context, Peter and John are on trial before a council investigating their message and ministry. Perhaps the disciples were not formally trained in the same kind of religious training that their interrogators were, but this does not mean that they were bumbling backwater hillbillies. Somehow, their critics overlooked three continuous years of formal and informal training with Jesus Christ, which apparently only qualified for them as being "uneducated". As we know all too well in our day of political and media spin, opponents are also prone to lie. The claim that Peter was "uneducated" may have been simply ancient fake news seeking to destroy his credibility as a public leader for Christ, which would be nothing new. In the same way, Charles Spurgeon, one of the greatest Bible teachers in the history of the church, was not formally theologically educated, and would therefore not pass the ordination requirements in most denominations that share his Reformed theological convictions. Funny enough, he is often quoted and read in theology schools where he would also not qualify as a professor because he was "uneducated" and "common". Yet, he is one of the greatest Bible teachers in world history.

We simply do not know about Peter's education. Even if he was not formally educated, it does not logically follow that he was unintelligent. After all, the Wright brothers who brought us the plane, author Mark Twain, primatologist Jane Goodall, legendary scientist Michael Faraday, microbiology founder Anton Van Leeuwenhoek, Declaration of Independence co-author Benjamin Franklin, automobile inventor Henry Ford, slave educator Frederick Douglas, genetics pioneer Gregor Mendel, discipline changing mathematician Srinivas Ramanujan, businessman John Rockefeller, astronaut John Glenn, along with computer innovator Bill Gates, and Jesus Christ who formally taught Peter for three years all had one thing in common – they never graduated from college. Mass murderer Ted Bundy did graduate college with distinction, however, and went on to law school. The point is that you can be intelligent even if you don't go to college, and if you do go to college it doesn't guarantee you are intelligent.

3. 1 Peter 5:12 reveals something very important to understanding the authorship of that book, "By Silvanus, a faithful brother as I

regard him, I have written briefly to you, exhorting and declaring that this is the true grace of God. Stand firm in it." We are not told exactly what part Silvanus played in the writing or editing of the letter, but the fact he is mentioned reveals that at the very least, Paul was not writing completely alone. In Acts 15:22, Silvanus (also called Silas) is chosen for significant public ministry as one of the most trusted men in the early church. In 2 Corinthians 1:19, Paul also mentions Silvanus along with Timothy as his leadership team. In 1 Thessalonians 1:1 and 2 Thessalonians 2:1, Paul mentions Silvanus along with Timothy yet again as editors and/or co-authors of that book of the Bible. Like Michael Jordan, perhaps Peter succeeded in his writing and ministry because he had surrounded himself with an incredible team to complement and complete him?

4. In argumentation, there is something called the burden of proof. Practically, this means that if someone presents a clear case, then the critic of that case has the burden of disproving it and dislodging it with a better case for another outcome. It is easy to criticize someone's position, but unless you've got a better idea then that idea should stand. Here's the case that 1-2 Peter makes for the authorship of Peter:
    - 1 Peter 1:1 – Peter, an apostle of Jesus Christ."
    - 1 Peter 5:1 – ...a fellow elder and a witness of the sufferings of Christ.
    - 2 Peter 1:1 – Simeon Peter, a servant and apostle of Jesus Christ.
    - 2 Peter 1:16–18 – For we did not follow cleverly devised myths when we made known to you the power and coming of our Lord Jesus Christ, but we were eyewitnesses of his majesty. For when he received honor and glory from God the Father, and the voice was borne to him by the Majestic Glory, "This is my beloved Son, with whom I am well pleased," we ourselves heard this very voice borne from heaven, for we were with him on the holy mountain.
    - 2 Peter 3:1 – This is now the second letter that I am writing to you, beloved.
    - 2 Peter 3:15-16 – Our beloved brother Paul also wrote

to you according to the wisdom given him, as he does in all his letters when he speaks in them of these matters. There are some things in them that are hard to understand, which the ignorant and unstable twist to their own destruction, as they do the other Scriptures.

If the author is not Peter, then who is the author in light of this impressive list of reasons to believe the simple fact that it's Peter? Perhaps another author is possible, but who in the world could be considered probable other than Peter? Who else is one of the 12 apostles chosen by Jesus, a well-known early church leader, suffered and served for Christ, were eyewitnesses to Jesus' earthly ministry, was one of the few people on the Mount of Transfiguration when God the Father spoke from heaven, also wrote 2 Peter in addition to 1 Peter, was close friends with Paul, and had the spiritual authority to confirm Paul's writings as "Scripture"?

5. Additionally, Bible commentators who have studied the issue point out that the early church leaders like Clement of Alexandria, Tertullian, Polycarp, and Irenaeus considered Peter to have been the author of the two books bearing his name. Renowned Bible Commentator F.F. Bruce says, "1 Peter... was never doubted by the early Church."[8] New Testament scholar D. A. Carson calls Paul Achtemeier's commentary on 1 Peter "the fullest commentary in English at the exegetical level" and "a masterpiece of careful scholarship."[9] The scholar Achtemeier concludes after exhaustive and arguably unprecedented research, "The majority of the evidence, both external and internal, would appear to support the traditional view that Peter the apostle wrote this letter."[10]

Lastly, the unique claim of the Bible is that its books have dual authorship. In addition to the human author, there is God the Holy Spirit at work in and through the human author empowering them to communicate perfectly. Peter himself acknowledges this fact about Old Testament books written by human authors because of "the Spirit of Christ in them" (1 Peter 1:11) as they "spoke from God as they were carried along by the Holy Spirit" (2 Peter 1:21). Peter extends the principle of dual authorship to New Testament books speaking of

"Paul" who "wrote to you according to the wisdom given him" by the Holy Spirit in his New Testament "letters" which are divine "Scriptures". The storyline of the Bible is that brush in the desert does not talk to people, shepherd boys don't kill warrior giants, raging seas don't suddenly part for fleeing multitudes, bread does not show up outside a million tents simultaneously year after year every morning, dead people don't rise, and perfect books don't get written...unless God shows up. Then, everything changes. If you add the Holy Spirit to the life of Peter, then it's not hard to believe how he got everything done including writing two books of the Bible.

CHAPTER 2

GETTING FAMILIAR WITH THE LETTER OF 1 PETER

"This epistle of Peter is one of the grandest of the New Testament, and it is the true, pure gospel. For Peter...inculcates the true doctrine of faith—how Christ has been given to us, who takes away our sins and saves us."

— Martin Luther

In our day of short texts, spam emails, and social media responses of merely an emoji, it's quite a treat to get a hand-written lengthy personal letter from someone you love. There is something special about getting such a personal and thoughtful correspondence and explains why everything from birthday cards to love letters and letters from the frontlines of war are among most people's most treasured possessions.

The Bible is essentially a library grouped by genre of literature. Much of the New Testament is hand-written letters that were delivered across many miles long before the current ease of sending and receiving mail and packages. Generally speaking, the letters were an incredible honor for a church to receive from someone like Paul or Peter. The entire church would gather, the letter would be opened, and the Word from God would be read aloud to the church family, often meeting in homes.

The authors of these New Testament letters functioned a lot like dads, which is the essence of apostolic leadership. The churches they oversaw were like families, and as good dads often do, they would call a family meeting and write a letter in cases where they could not be physically present to lead the family. The content of those letters is the same things that pastors concern themselves with today – false teachers that need to be rebuked, sinners that need to be corrected, new Christians that need to be instructed, hurting people who need to be encouraged, and divided people who need to be reconciled.

Peter's two letters are a mere 166 verses. Although rather brief, they are power packed. The people he wrote to were living in a pagan city which meant that to live as a Christian made them the oddballs. Making matters worse, they were facing a host of troubles, trials, and temptations among uncertain days filled with distressing difficulty. Peter had experienced all of these things himself and watched first-hand how to respond by being at the side of Jesus for three years. So, he writes from his own experience and points people to Jesus for hope, help, and healing.

We tend to think of one church meeting in many locations as something new, but it is not. In our day, just as in the early days of the church, God gives some people apostolic gifting that allows them to lead multiple churches and pastor many pastors. As the opening lines of 1 Peter indicate, he is writing to a multi-campus church scattered over a wide geographic region. The ancient cities of "Pontus, Galatia, Cappadocia, Asia, and Bithynia" were located in modern-day Turkey which, sadly, is now the least churched nation in the world, a fact I can verify after preaching in that nation on a few trips.

Commenting on the size of the region to which Peter writes, Bible commentator Karen Jobes says, "This is a vast area of approximately 129,000 square miles...(As a comparison, the state of California covers about 159,000 square miles.)"[11]

She goes on to say, "The residents practiced many religions, spoke several languages, and were never really assimilated into the Greco-Roman culture...And yet this untamed region became the cradle of Christianity...We may surmise that, in no small part because of this letter [1 Peter] and the faithfulness of those who received it, well-established churches flourished in all five of these regions by AD 180. Their bishops attended the great councils of the second through the fourth centuries, where the doctrines were forged that Christians hold dear yet today."[12]

WHERE AND WHEN 1-2 PETER WERE WRITTEN

When we receive a hand-written letter or card in the mail, the first things we tend to do are check where it was from and who wrote it. The same is true in studying a letter in the Bible. We've already established that Peter wrote it. Now, we will consider when and where he penned it from.

In 1 Peter 5:13, Peter says he is writing from "Babylon" but the language is probably metaphorical rather than referring to the former capital of Nebuchadnezzar's empire. Hundreds of years prior, Babylon was a godless place that held and abused God's people for some seventy years until, in the days of Daniel, God liberated them. Returning there for no reason would be like a formerly tortured prisoner of war taking a long journey some 700 miles back to the cell of their torment to simply hang out. It makes no sense. Babylon was the last place God's people wanted to be and was for Jews at that time the same kind of place that an abandoned concentration camp would be for Jews today. Furthermore, by Peter's time, the ancient city of Babylon was a sparsely inhabited ruin as God had promised (Isaiah 14:23). In Revelation 16:19 and 17:5, "Babylon" is used as a cryptic name for Rome, and Colossians 4:10 and Philemon 24 (most likely written in Rome) show that Mark was already there with Paul. Babylon was as bad as it got and therefore became the nickname for any godless forsaken place.

The reason that ancient Babylon and later Rome are called "Babylon" is because the same demonic spirit was at work in both places seeking to establish a counterfeit kingdom to war against the Kingdom of God. This also explains why at the end of history, Revelation 14:8 reports, "Fallen, fallen is Babylon the great, she who made all nations drink the wine of the passion of her sexual immorality." Revelation 17:5 speaks of "Babylon the great, mother of prostitutes and of earth's abominations." Revelation 18:2 says, "Fallen, fallen is Babylon the great! She has become a dwelling place for demons, a haunt for every unclean spirit..." Behind all godless worldly demonic culture from sexual sin to the porn industry, human trafficking and drug and alcohol addictions, along with cartels and crime syndicates propped up by godless governments is a demonic spirit named Babylon. Once Jesus returns to destroy her, all that she has created crumbles. When Peter says he's writing from Babylon, he's making it clear the church is up against a godless, demonic culture.

In 2 Timothy 4:11, we also find Mark in Asia Minor, and Paul sends for him to come, most probably to Rome, the new "Babylon". The fact that neither Peter nor Paul mentions the other in the list of those invited to Rome indicates that the men were together at the time of writing their letters. These lines of evidence help strengthen the case that Peter wrote from Rome, something the church fathers Tertullian and Eusebius also state as fact.[13]

Concerning the timing of the writing of 1-2 Peter, a date during the reign of the godless ruler Nero (AD 54–68) is considered by many scholars the most likely timeframe. Since Peter makes no reference to Paul's martyrdom that likely happened when persecution broke out against Christians in Rome in 64 AD, 1 Peter was most likely written before then. The death of Paul would have been something worthy of note and so the silence is telling. Furthermore, that Peter encourages Christians to submit to the Emperor seems most likely before Christians were being slaughtered as martyrs (1 Peter 2:13). The most common summary conclusion among Bible scholars is that 1-2 Peter were written somewhere around AD 63–64.

This timing of Nero's reign as Caesar would also make sense of the need for Peter to write to the church about their "fiery trial" (1 Peter 4:12). This was most likely prophetic in advance, or less likely but also possibly in response to current events in that day.

A Bible encyclopedia explains, "In AD 64 a fire broke out...in Rome. It spread quickly, devouring everything in its path. Fanned by the wind, it raged for more than five days and devastated a large area of the city before being brought under control. At the time Nero was at...his birthplace, some 33 miles to the south. He rushed to Rome to organize relief work. Because of his evil record, however, people put stock in the rumor that Nero had set the fire himself.

Nero, in turn, found a scapegoat in the Christians, whom he charged with the crime. Many were persecuted. Perhaps the apostle Peter in his first letter was referring to the sufferings of Christians during the last few years of Nero's reign (1 Pt 4:12)...The church had increased in numbers and had become a movement. Tacitus alluded to the size of the church when he wrote that 'a huge crowd was convicted not so much of arson as of hatred of the human race.'

It is likely that Peter and Paul were executed during the Neronian persecution. Clement of Rome, an early church father, in his letter to the church at Corinth (written presumably in AD 95), referred to the heroes of faith 'who lived nearest to our time,' namely Peter and Paul, who suffered martyrdom."[14]

Before the persecution of Christians arose, there was a growing undercurrent of disdain for Christians that paved the way for persecution. Those are the underlying reasons that 1-2 Peter were written.

WHY 1-2 PETER WERE WRITTEN

Imagine you lived a few thousand years ago, hundreds of miles away from someone, and the only way to communicate with them was to sit down and write a letter, and then find someone to hand deliver it to them by walking or riding on the back of a beast for many days through rough terrain.

How many letters would you send? The odds are, few, if any.

For someone as busy as Peter, to sit down and write a letter to then have it delivered would indicate that the people he was writing to had a deep need that only his wise counsel could most help. The fact that such letters were written by the apostles, and delivered by trusted members of their ministry teams, reveals the great love they had for people with great need.

The churches and Christians who received Peter's letter would have been tremendously honored and encouraged at the willingness of such a noteworthy Christian leader to take the time, although he had never even met them, to speak into their life with practical pastoral affection. Imagine, for example, finding an old letter to your local church hand-written by Billy Graham revealing in great detail his knowledge and love for the people. Also, the fact that Peter took the time to pen not one, but two letters, indicates that there were serious concerns that had escalated to the point of urgency.

The original audience of 1 Peter was a suffering audience. Like all of us, they had trials, troubles, and temptations that threatened to exhaust them until they defeated them. What was the nature of this suffering? Jobes writes, "Virtually all commentators understand the persecutions referred to in 1 Peter to be sporadic, personal, and unorganized social ostracism of Christians with varying intensity, probably reinforced at the local level by the increasing suspicions of Roman officials at all levels."[15]

Bible commentator Paul Achtemeier agrees that the persecution in 1 Peter is, "due more to unofficial harassment than to official policy, more local than regional, and more at the initiation of the general populace as the result of a reaction against the lifestyle of the Christians than at the initiation of Roman officials because of some general policy of seeking out and punishing Christians. That does not rule out the possibility that persecutions occurred over large areas of the empire; they surely did, but they were spasmodic and broke out at different times in different places, the result of the flare up of local hatreds rather than because Roman officials were engaged in the regular discharge of official policy."[16]

Peter's underlying concern was about what we today call tolerance, diversity, and religious pluralism that discriminates against Christianity in a way that is intolerant, not diverse, and religious persecution. Subsequently, 1-2 Peter, although a few thousand years old, are incredibly timely to our current culture in which Christians are welcome to love Jesus so long as they agree that other religions and spiritualities are equally valid, do nothing to discourage others from patronizing their spiritualities and religions by speaking against them or evangelizing people, and are willing to actively participate as requested with practitioners of other religions and spiritualities so as to be loving, tolerant, and non-judgmental in the eyes of the world. The struggle is real, but not really new.

Christianity spread to the region where Peter's letter was originally sent as those converted to Jesus at the Pentecost holiday sermon preached by Peter (Acts 2:9) after returning to their hometowns. Following regeneration by God the Holy Spirit, their minds, desires, and actions changed, which made them unpopular with mainstream culture. If you meet Jesus later in life, as I did in college, you quickly find that most everything the average person does for fun on a weekend is breaking the 10 Commandments. So, you've got a choice to make if you want to stick with Team Jesus with the jeers or join Team Judas with the cheers.

The Christians writing to Peter would have looked to him as something of a spiritual father. Born again under his preaching, they look to Peter like a young kid does a good dad, seeking advice on how to live life.

The unpopularity of Christians was in large part due to the fact that their moral conduct had changed. A hypocrite Christian is a hero, but a holy Christian is a zero. The Christians were no longer willing to eat too much, drink too much, party sinfully, or engage in sex outside of marriage (1 Peter 4:1–4). Those who had previously known them and enjoyed sinning with them prior to their conversion considered their life change negatively. The drinking buddies who lost their wingmen and the boyfriends who got dumped by their live-in girlfriends who walked away to walk with Jesus were not pleased with the influence Christianity was having on their friends. Jesus is a real buzzkill to weekend plans for dating, relating, drinking, and fornicating.

The unpopularity of Christians was also due to the fact that their devotion to Jesus above everyone and everything else caused them to be viewed as subversives overturning long-held familial and cultural norms. Simply, once people became Christians, their lifestyle changed and they stopped worshiping the gods of their empire, city, trade guild, or family. This can feel like rejection to former friends and family, and repudiation of deeply held cultural expectations. Jesus freaks are always the oddballs and outcasts no matter where they live.

In that day, paying religious homage to the gods and goddesses of the nation was akin to waving a flag or saying the pledge of allegiance in our cultural context. So, when the Christians refused to participate in any religious homage, worship, or devotion to the state gods, they were seen as unpatriotic. Why? Once they pledged allegiance to King Jesus, all other former loyalties were severed.

Cities had their own gods and goddesses who were honored in various city-wide events as a unifying way of bringing diverse people together. When Christians refused to be involved in any city-wide events that included honoring gods and goddesses other than Jesus Christ, they were seen as judgmentally too-serious bad neighbors. Today, this would be the equivalent of not getting drunk on New Year's Eve, not trading beads for britches on Mardi Gras, and not getting drunk and cursing out grandmothers from the other team while tailgating on game day when, up to this point, these things comprised every photo on your social media page.

Various professions were also held together by trade guilds, akin to our unions, that included meetings with religious rites and ceremonies dedicated to various gods and goddesses. When Christians refused to participate in the religious aspects of their trade guild, they were considered unprofessional. They were even demoted or terminated from their jobs, suffering financial loss for their unyielding devotion to Jesus Christ. It may seem shocking to us that unless you worship a demon the union can fire you. Just try working at Planned Parenthood after you stop worshipping the Old Testament God of child sacrifice named Molech, start worshipping Jesus as God, and see how long you keep your job. Jobs change, and labor unions change, but demons working through them stay the same.

Furthermore, families were held together in large part by religious traditions that included holiday parties and meals dedicated to various gods and goddesses who were honored by the family at both home and temple events. When Christians refused to participate in these kinds of holiday events, they were considered disrespectful to their families. Today, examples would include new Christians from Japanese homes who refuse to worship their ancestors, converts from Native American spirituality who refuse to join their family in worshipping demonic spirits in animals and nature, and anyone who comes from a family that worships alcohol, the family business, a political party, or a sports team with religious zeal and simply loses interest in those things because Jesus is enough for them.

HOW 1-2 PETER RELATE TO US TODAY

While it is easy to think that the Bible is old and outdated, the truth is that since God doesn't change, and people don't change, the Bible is timeless and therefore timely for everyone everywhere. In Peter's day, like our own, the average person's commitment to their version of spirituality was very shallow and nowhere near the deep end of the pool. Their spiritual beliefs, like ours, were simply part of the cultural tradition to keep up social status and little more. Christians, however, challenged these assumptions with deep devotion to Jesus and were thought to be too serious about their Jesus. Some modern-day examples might help illuminate the spirt of why Peter wrote his letters.

One woman was raised in a family that celebrated Halloween as a major holiday, complete with her parents' home being decorated up with witches, skeletons, spider webs, zombies, demons, and more. The entire family would gather at the home dressed up as witches, warlocks, and the like to hand out candy to the neighborhood children. They also set up a false graveyard and a small haunted house in which they showed fake murders and other things intended to frighten children. Upon her conversion, the woman (who was by this time a mother with her own young children) refused to dress up like a witch, dress her daughter up like a demon ghost, and participate with her extended family in their annual Halloween celebration. As a result, her family regularly criticized her, exerting pressure on her to coexist with the rest of the family by violating her Christian conscience.

A man who was baptized as an infant in a very dead church grew up as a non-Christian whose family virtually never entered church other than for weddings and funerals. Later in life, he met Jesus and grew quickly as a Bible-believing Christian. He married a godly woman and God blessed them with a healthy, beautiful baby boy. His non-Christian parents pressured him to have the baby baptized in the church they never attended as a sort of superstitious rite; they wrongly believed that by baptizing the baby in that building he would automatically go to heaven if he died as an infant. The man lovingly tried to explain to his parents that he would do no such thing because it was not his church and he did not share their beliefs. Eventually, the entire extended family formed something of an alliance against him, as each of them had had their own children baptized in the parents' church even though none of them was living as a Christian. He lovingly and graciously held his ground but was in many ways ostracized by his entire family and his deeply hurt parents even threatened to cut him out of his inheritance for dishonoring them.

The threat that Peter responds to is one that we face in our own day - that Christians will fold under trial. Peter understood this well as he was a bit of an evanjellyfish with no spiritual vertebrae, until God repeatedly put some steel in his spine. As 2 Timothy 3:12 promises, "Indeed, all who desire to live a godly life in Christ Jesus will be persecuted." Sometimes persecution is life-threatening, or even life-taking. This degree of persecution broke out a few years after Peter penned his letters, when the madman Emperor Nero burned Christians alive as torches for his parties, threw them into the arena to be killed by gladiators and eaten by lions, and killed their pastors including Paul and Peter. In this way, Peter's reference to "fiery trials" may in fact have been a very literal prophetic warning of impending persecution. Still, the kind of persecution faced by Christians is more frequently the kind that 1 and 2 Peter address.

In a word, the Christians were marginalized as weirdos. They were weirdos who loved Jesus so much that they lived their lives and viewed their faith in a way that made them holy, or different, than other people. What God calls holy the world calls weird. What God calls good the world calls odd. Because they would not get drunk, sleep around, or practice other religions and spiritualities—or even endorse such things by their approval—they were viewed by everyone else as basically just plain weird, odd, and way too serious Jesus Freaks.

Subsequently, the Christians suffered shame, family rejection, discrimination, mockery, half-truths, lies, vicious rumors, slander, harassment, abuse, economic persecution, rejection, and mob violence on occasion, although such persecution was likely not yet state-sponsored. Basically, Christians stepped out to live with, for, like, and to Jesus. In response, the world pushed back and tried to get them to go back in the closet with a private faith that did not affect their external life or allow them to make any cultural changes. Thus, and this point is vital to a correct understanding of Peter's letters, they were suffering not because of their sin but rather because of their faithful devotion to Jesus. One lesson we learn from Jesus is that not everyone who gets in trouble did something bad.

However, the Christians were wavering in their devotion. Like so many college students who are weary of being mocked by their professors for being Bible-believing Christians and getting their grades reduced, husbands who are mocked by their buddies for not looking at porn or partying with their coworkers after work, wives who forego a professional career to stay at home to be a wife and mother, virgin singles who are the punchline of jokes at the gym for waiting until marriage to have sex, and net surfers who can't stomach one more nasty blog or negative news story about their faith and church, their resolve was tried. Various people were pulled in a variety of directions:

1. Some were enticed by the liberal route of compromise to not eliminate their Bible as much as edit it. They wanted to cut out—or at least explain away—the parts of the Bible that they were being criticized for believing. In our day, this would be most typified by the mainline

liberal Christian denominations with pastors who endorse all religions and spiritualities and officiate marriages between any genders, under the oversight of unsaved bishops who appreciate their tolerance, pluralism, and minds so open that their brains fall out. This is one of the central issues at the heart of 2 Peter.

2. Some were compelled to privatize their faith. Sure, in private they would pray to and worship Jesus. But in public they would shut their mouths and keep their faith to themselves so as to not be considered the weirdo for Jesus. Some were closet Christians.
3. Some were considering abandoning their faith altogether. They were tired of being the butt of jokes in the press and on the late-night talk shows and wearied of being the laughingstock Jesus Freaks. Why? Because most people simply do not like being the oddball, misfit, and outcast—especially those who are young and want to be cool and those who are old with privileged social positions to uphold and lifestyles to fund. Our day is like theirs. Carrying a Bible around is about as socially acceptable as walking around with your underwear outside your pants.
4. Still others were attracted to the fighting posture of religious fundamentalism. They were preparing to separate from the culture, set up their own subculture, defend themselves, and talk trash about the non-Christians who were criticizing them, all in the name of a culture war. In the fight or flight cycle, these are the fighters who declare Jihad for Jesus.

If any of these four options were chosen by the churches Peter writes to, it would have simply died in one way or another. The work of Jesus would have stopped in that region and so Peter had to help them navigate living their faith in a hostile culture. So, Peter opens by calling Christians "elect exiles". Elect meant they were chosen by God. Exiles meant they were far away from their Heavenly Home. Sent as missionaries, although hated by the culture, they were to bring the culture of Heaven to lost people in hopes that love, grace, mercy, and forgiveness would see people saved and culture changed. Our mission and message remain the same.

HOW THE FIRST CHRISTIANS FACED WHAT YOU DO

Most non-Christians see Christians as odd. Giving your money to God is odd. Not having sex outside of marriage is odd. Not getting drunk or high is odd. Forgiving your enemy is odd. And, having a personal relationship with someone you cannot see sounds like kids having an imaginary friend, and that's really odd.

Conversely, living in this world as a Christian is odd for us. Paying for insurance that covers murdering babies but not taking vitamins is odd. Paying the public schools to undermine most of your values is odd. Paying for politicians to erode your freedoms to live out your faith is odd. Seeing the rainbow God chose as the sign of the Noahic covenant to never flood this sinful planet again is odd to see on guys dressed up like the Village People. Constantly being invited to pride parades, the very problem that got Satan kicked out of heaven and unleashed hell on the earth, is also odd.

Living as a Christian, feeling odd, in a world that considers you odd, is an odd place to be. This is why 1 Peter was written and why we need to study it. After years of wearing a reversible jersey and repeatedly changing from Team Jesus to not Team Jesus, as a seasoned older man Peter had finally learned some lessons the hard way and was ready to coach the new members of Team Jesus. Peter's lesson is that our life is filled with troubles, trials and temptations that cause problems, pains, and perils. The good news, however, is that, like a gardener, God uses the manure of this world as fertilizer to increase the fruitfulness of our lives in four ways:

1. Your test is for your testimony.
   - "You have been grieved by various trials, so that the tested genuineness of your faith—more precious than gold that perishes though it is tested by fire—may be found to result in praise and glory and honor at the revelation of Jesus Christ." (1 Peter 1:6–7)
   - "Beloved, do not be surprised at the fiery trial when it comes upon you to test you, as though something

strange were happening to you." (1 Peter 4:12)

- "The Lord knows how to rescue the godly from trials." (2 Peter 2:9)

2. When people judge you, don't worry as Jesus will judge them and vindicate you.
   - "And if you call on him as Father who judges impartially according to each one's deeds, conduct yourselves with fear throughout the time of your exile." (1 Peter 1:17)
   - "They will give account to him who is ready to judge the living and the dead." (1 Peter 4:5)
   - "And after you have suffered a little while, the God of all grace, who has called you to his eternal glory in Christ, will himself restore, confirm, strengthen, and establish you." (1 Peter 5:10)
   - "But rejoice insofar as you share Christ's sufferings, that you may also rejoice and be glad when his glory is revealed." (1 Peter 4:13)
3. Don't treat them as they treat you, treat them as He treats you.
   - "When he was reviled, he did not revile in return; when he suffered, he did not threaten, but continued entrusting himself to him who judges justly." (1 Peter 2:23)
   - "Keep your conduct among the Gentiles honorable, so that when they speak against you as evildoers, they may see your good deeds and glorify God on the day of visitation." (1 Peter 2:12)
   - "In your hearts honor Christ the Lord as holy, always being prepared to make a defense to anyone who asks you for a reason for the hope that is in you; yet do it with gentleness and respect, having a good conscience, so that, when you are slandered, those who revile your good behavior in Christ may be put to shame." (1 Peter 3:15–16)
4. This is as close to hell as you will ever get, so keep going 'til you're Home.
   - ". . . in the sanctification of the Spirit, for obedience to

Jesus Christ . . ." (1 Peter 1:2)

- "In this you rejoice, though now for a little while, if necessary, you have been grieved by various trials, so that the tested genuineness of your faith—more precious than gold that perishes though it is tested by fire—may be found to result in praise and glory and honor at the revelation of Jesus Christ. Though you have not seen him, you love him. Though you do not now see him, you believe in him and rejoice with joy that is inexpressible and filled with glory." (1 Peter 1:6–8)
- "His divine power has granted to us all things that pertain to life and godliness, through the knowledge of him who called us to his own glory and excellence." (2 Peter 1:3)
- "But grow in the grace and knowledge of our Lord and Savior Jesus Christ. To him be the glory both now and to the day of eternity. Amen." (2 Peter 3:18)

To encourage someone is to put courage into them. At some point, every Christian needs courage to continue to stand up for Christ in our falling down world. You need courage if you want to live with, for, and like Christ. The Perfect Spirit says it perfectly through the imperfect Peter, "My purpose in writing is to encourage you and assure you that what you are experiencing is truly part of God's grace for you. Stand firm in this grace" (1 Peter 5:12 NLT). Like any soldier in a battle, you need to stand firm and hold your ground until you see Jesus coming on the clouds of Heaven riding a white horse wielding His sword to end the battle. For those who want it, God's grace is available to put steel in your spine as it did Peter. Life is odd. God is good. That's the message of Peter.

CHAPTER 3

A 9-PART STUDY OF 1 PETER FOR INDIVIDUALS AND GROUPS

The following study guide is intended to help individuals and groups learn 1 Peter. Please use this guide as tools and not rules. As the Holy Spirit guides your time in Scripture, and as you have discussion with others, the goal is not finishing the guide but rather meeting with God through learning the Bible. Consider this guide more as a compass pointing you in a direction than a map that directs your every step. For example, most weeks there will be more questions for the Talk it Out section than can be covered in one group time together, and this is intentional so that people can choose the questions they find most helpful from a menu of options. The format for each week lays out as follows:

1. Scripture for each week
2. Introduction and overview of each week's Scripture
3. Think it out: Questions for personal study
4. Talk it out: Questions for group discussion
5. Walk it out: Questions for personal action
6. Pray it out: Ways for group members to pray together

WEEK 1: 1 PETER 1:1-12

Scripture:

[1]1 Peter, an apostle of Jesus Christ, To those who are elect
exiles of the Dispersion in Pontus, Galatia, Cappadocia, Asia, and
Bithynia, [2]according to the foreknowledge of God the Father, in the
sanctification of the Spirit, for obedience to Jesus Christ and for

sprinkling with his blood:

May grace and peace be multiplied to you. [3]Blessed be the God and Father of our Lord Jesus Christ! According to his great mercy, he has caused us to be born again to a living hope through the resurrection of Jesus Christ from the dead, [4]to an inheritance that is imperishable, undefiled, and unfading, kept in heaven for you, [5]who by God's power are being guarded through faith for a salvation ready to be revealed in the last time. [6]In this you rejoice, though now for a little while, if necessary, you have been grieved by various trials, [7]so that the tested genuineness of your faith—more precious than gold that perishes though it is tested by fire—may be found to result in praise and glory and honor at the revelation of Jesus Christ. [8]Though you have not seen him, you love him. Though you do not now see him, you believe in him and rejoice with joy that is inexpressible and filled with glory, [9]obtaining the outcome of your faith, the salvation of your souls. [10]Concerning this salvation, the prophets who prophesied about the grace that was to be yours searched and inquired carefully, [11]inquiring what person or time the Spirit of Christ in them was indicating when he predicted the sufferings of Christ and the subsequent glories. [12]It was revealed to them that they were serving not themselves but you, in the things that have now been announced to you through those who preached the good news to you by the Holy Spirit sent from heaven, things into which angels long to look.

Introduction and overview:

Peter opens by reminding believers in numerous local churches scattered across a geographic area that is a bit smaller than California that they belong to God. The Christians are struggling because their new lifestyle causes their non-Christian family, friends, and neighbors to consider them odd, which leads to social strain that makes life hard. Living as the outcast, oddball, and misfit can be discouraging and is the case for faithful Christians in every time and place. To provide hope and encouragement, Peter focuses attention from the painful realities of life to our personal relationship with God. Over our lives, we are told, is a good and powerful God who uses all of life, including the toughest trials, to make us like Jesus. This life is preparation for our eternal life in a Kingdom where we live out our deepest desires and are rewarded forever for faithfulness in this life.

This uniquely Christian view of God and life allows us to find peace and purpose in every circumstance, giving us strength to press onward as we follow Jesus' example on our way Home. Our joy and hope are not tied to the roller coaster of our circumstances, but rather our steady and dependable loving, secure, gracious relationship with a God who is with us and for us forever.

Think it out: Questions for personal study

1. Like a parent adopting a child, individual choosing their spouse, or person choosing their best friend, how special is it that God has elected, or chosen, you for a loving relationship that never ends?
2. Verse one calls the elect "exiles" (sometimes translated "strangers" or "aliens"). What does it mean to be an exile or an alien in your nation and culture?
3. What does verse two say about the purpose of our election?
4. What does verse three mean by saying that a person is not born a Christian but must be born again to be a Christian? (You may want to also look up John 3:1-16 to learn more about this).
5. How do the persons of the Trinity participate in this purpose? Look for the Father, Son, and Spirit in these verses.
6. Read Exodus 24:1–8. What is the significance of sprinkling with blood?
7. What were the Old Testament prophets trying to discern, and how were their writings inspired of God?

Talk it out: Questions for group discussion

1. Since the letter was written to numerous churches scattered across a wide geographic area, what does Peter model for us about the importance of unity and love across all Bible-believing, Jesus-loving Christian churches?
2. What does it mean practically to be citizens of the Kingdom of God while we are residents of a nation?
3. Peter brought the gospel to the people he writes to. Who brought the gospel to you?
4. How did God cause you to be born again?
5. How does the fire of trial purify the quality of our faith and inheritance like the smelter process does gold?

6. How does knowing that our life only improves after this life ends change our view of struggles, suffering, and sadness in this life?

Walk it out: Questions for personal action

1. How does the idea of being an alien—a citizen of a different kingdom—resonate? How does it feel unfamiliar, or actually make sense of how you feel, in this world?
2. Where have you become too "at home" in this world?
3. What is the living hope into which we are born? Why is the resurrection so significant with regard to our hope in Jesus?
4. How does Peter describe our inheritance? What is the significance of the words "imperishable," "undefiled," and "unfading"?
5. To what does Peter attribute the purpose of trials in our life?
6. How does our tested faith result in glory and honor?
7. What does it look like for hope to transform the way you live?
8. How have you seen your faith tested and Christ glorified through trials in your life?
9. How is the love for Jesus and joy of Jesus mentioned in verse eight manifested in your life?
10. Describe a time when you have gone to Scripture for comfort in the middle of a trial and found peace in God?

Pray it out: Ways for group members to pray together

1. What other churches can we be praying for so that there is unity across the Church in the local churches?
2. What non-Christian family or friends need to be born again that we can be praying for?
3. What tempting things in this world are hard for you to walk away from and you could use prayer and help for?
4. Is there any trial of note in your life right now (e.g. health issues, relational strain, job loss, stress, etc.)?
5. Peter was a spiritual leader trying to lead and feed God's people. Which spiritual leaders can you be praying for in support of them?

WEEK 2: 1 PETER 1:13-25

Scripture:

[13]Therefore, preparing your minds for action, and being sober-minded, set your hope fully on the grace that will be brought to you at the revelation of Jesus Christ. [14]As obedient children, do not be conformed to the passions of your former ignorance, [15]but as he who called you is holy, you also be holy in all your conduct, [16]since it is written, "You shall be holy, for I am holy." [17]And if you call on him as Father who judges impartially according to each one's deeds, conduct yourselves with fear throughout the time of your exile, [18]knowing that you were ransomed from the futile ways inherited from your forefathers, not with perishable things such as silver or gold, [19]but with the precious blood of Christ, like that of a lamb without blemish or spot. [20]He was foreknown before the foundation of the world but was made manifest in the last times for the sake of you [21]who through him are believers in God, who raised him from the dead and gave him glory, so that your faith and hope are in God. [22]Having purified your souls by your obedience to the truth for a sincere brotherly love, love one another earnestly from a pure heart, [23]since you have been born again, not of perishable seed but of imperishable, through the living and abiding word of God; [24]for "All flesh is like grass and all its glory like the flower of grass. The grass withers, and the flower falls, [25]but the word of the Lord remains forever." And this word is the good news that was preached to you.

Introduction and overview:

Early in his letter, Peter puts the focus on the person and work of Jesus Christ. In doing so, Peter is showing us the very practical ways that God's love has been given to us through Jesus, the difference He makes in our life, and the fact that we are not alone in life's struggles but rather have a God who has endured hardship and walks with us through ours. Furthermore, Jesus gave us the Bible as a trustworthy life-giving Word from God directing us how to live totally new lives that grow in holiness to be more like the Kingdom and less like the world.

Think it out: Questions for personal study

1. Reread verses 1-12 since the "therefore" in these Scriptures complete and apply the thoughts of the Scriptures that preceded it.
2. How does God's call to holiness rescue us from foolish and self-destructive patterns we inherit from our family according to verses 14-18?
3. In verse 19 there is a quote from Exodus 12:5 in reference to the Passover where God's people demonstrated faith in Jesus coming by sacrificing an unblemished lamb for their sins so that death and wrath would pass over them. Read Exodus 12 to better understand Jesus' death on the cross for you.
4. Make a list of all the things these verses teach about what Jesus Christ did to save sinners.
5. Make a list of all the things these verses teach about the perfection and power of Scripture.
6. Verses 24-25 are a quotation from Isaiah 40 that prophecy hundreds of years in advance that John the Baptizer would come to prepare the way for Jesus Christ to fulfill the Scriptures. Read Isaiah 40 to get a sense of the greatness of God.

Talk it out: Questions for group discussion

1. What are the practical ways you can "prepare your minds for action" like in verse 13?
2. What are some self-destructive and foolish ways from prior generations of your family that God has ransomed and rescued you from?
3. What does holiness, or practical changes in your life, look like for you?
4. What is your favorite thing that Peter teaches about Jesus in this section of Scripture? Why?
5. According to verse 22, our loving relationship with Jesus should cause us to love other Christians like family – which Christians have loved you well?
6. Peter makes some big statements about the Bible being trustworthy. Do you have any struggles accepting all of God's Word as trustworthy and true? If so, what parts or why?

Walk it out: Questions for personal action

1. Are your entertainment, news, and social media choices helping you prepare your mind for godly or ungodly action?
2. What patterns have you inherited from prior generations of your family that need to change for you to be healthy, holy, and happy?
3. Peter talks about God as our Father, and us as His beloved children. Is it easy or hard for you to relate to God as Father? Why? How can this relationship be improved?
4. Peter says your relationship with God is more valuable than anything – including your wealth (silver and gold) – do you really believe this, and do you show it by giving your wealth back to God generously?
5. How is your time in God's Word and is there any need or way for improvement in learning the Bible?
6. Peter says that the Bible is like a seed that gets planted and brings life. Who do you know that you need to give a Bible, or invite to church, so that the seed of God's Word can get planted in their soul?
7. When Peter uses words like "obedience", "holy", and "judges" is there any reason that something in you wants to bristle or push back that needs to be addressed?
8. Is there any Christian you need to do a better job of extending "a sincere brotherly love" and "love...earnestly from a pure heart"?
9. Since Jesus forgave you so that you could have a relationship with Him, is there any other person you need to forgive so that you can have a relationship with them?

Pray it out: Ways for group members to pray together

1. How can we pray that your relationship with God the Father improves?
2. How can we pray that your relationship with Jesus Christ improves?
3. How can we pray that your relationship with your family (forefathers) improves?
4. How can we pray that your relationship with fellow Christians improves?

5. How can we pray that your relationship with a non-Christian improves so you can help plant the seed of God's Word in their life?
6. How can we pray for your relationship with God's Word to improve?

WEEK 3: 1 PETER 2:1-12

Scripture:

1So put away all malice and all deceit and hypocrisy and envy and all slander. 2Like newborn infants, long for the pure spiritual milk, that by it you may grow up into salvation— 3if indeed you have tasted that the Lord is good. 4As you come to him, a living stone rejected by men but in the sight of God chosen and precious, 5you yourselves like living stones are being built up as a spiritual house, to be a holy priesthood, to offer spiritual sacrifices acceptable to God through Jesus Christ. 6For it stands in Scripture: "Behold, I am laying in Zion a stone, a cornerstone chosen and precious, and whoever believes in him will not be put to shame." 7So the honor is for you who believe, but for those who do not believe, "The stone that the builders rejected has become the cornerstone," 8and "A stone of stumbling, and a rock of offense." They stumble because they disobey the word, as they were destined to do. 9But you are a chosen race, a royal priesthood, a holy nation, a people for his own possession, that you may proclaim the excellencies of him who called you out of darkness into his marvelous light. 10Once you were not a people, but now you are God's people; once you had not received mercy, but now you have received mercy. 11Beloved, I urge you as sojourners and exiles to abstain from the passions of the flesh, which wage war against your soul. 12Keep your conduct among the Gentiles honorable, so that when they speak against you as evildoers, they may see your good deeds and glorify God on the day of visitation.

Introduction and overview:

God is a King with a Kingdom that the Bible refers to as "Zion". Today, God's Kingdom rules in the unseen realm, and Jesus taught us to pray and prepare for the day when God's Kingdom would come to earth, and God's will would be done without sin or exception. In the Old Testament, God's Kingdom/Zion was manifest on the earth with the holiest people who were the priests, and the holiest place which was the Temple. That was the connecting point between Heaven and earth, where sin was forgiven, lives were changed, families were healed, and joyful celebration was had. Peter extends these hopeful concepts to the life of every Christian as today our lives are God's Zion and Temple founded on Jesus Christ as the cornerstone upon which all our life is built so that God's grace transforms all of life!

Think it out: Questions for personal study

1. What is Peter's big idea when he says that we can get rid of the things that make us sick and unhealthy (malice, deceit, hypocrisy, envy, slander) and have a change in our spiritual diet that makes us healthy in God's goodness in verse 1?
2. Verse 6 quotes Isaiah 28:16. Read Isaiah 28 to learn about God's judgment upon those who reject Jesus no matter what nation or family they are from.
3. Verse 7 quotes Psalm 118:22. Read Psalm 118, which is one of the most hopeful chapters in the Bible about all the good things our loving God has in store for those who receive Jesus.
4. Verse 8 quotes Isaiah 8:14 and mentions Jesus as offensive to some people who trip over him and fall into harm. Read Isaiah 8:11-22 and look for the ways that people who reject Jesus try to control their life apart from God and fail.
5. Make a list of all the things God says you are in verses 9-11. How amazing is that list!
6. What is the heart of Peter's passionate plea for our behavior choices in verses 11-12? What are the good things God has for those who seek holiness?

Talk it out: Questions for group discussion

1. Since verse 7 quotes Psalm 118:22, have someone in the group read all of Psalm 118 aloud and sense the environment the Holy Spirit creates in your midst as faith rises up in the hearing of the Word of God.
2. What does it mean to practically have Jesus be the cornerstone of every area of your life (e.g. physical, mental, emotional, spiritual, financial, marital, parental, vocational, etc.)?
3. What are ways that you have seen people stumble over and be offended by Jesus like verse 8 says? How were you offended by and tripping over Jesus before you became a Christian?
4. What is your favorite thing that God says you are in verses 9-11? Why?

5. What are some very specific ways God has given you mercy in life like in verse 10?
6. What people are watching your life (child, spouse, family, friend, neighbor, coworker) and learning about your Jesus like verses 11-12 says?

Walk it out: Questions for personal action

1. What do you need to "put away" in your life once and for all?
2. In a very practical way, come up with examples that related to the comparison and contrast between things that fit into the categories that make you healthy versus make you sick in verses 1-2? What makes your soul sick (e.g. who are you unforgiving of, where are you being a hypocrite, who are you slandering, who do you envy)? What makes your soul healthy (e.g. Bible study, prayer, worship, service, evangelism, tithing, etc.)?
3. Is there any area of your life that is not fully founded on Jesus Christ as the beginning and cornerstone? What changes need to be made to remedy that liability?
4. What darkness is God calling you out of, and what light is God calling you into?
5. What specific passions of your flesh feel like a genuine war against your soul?
6. Where has Zion showed up in your life?
7. Is there any non-Christian you have sinned with or against that you need to apologize to so that they see God's love and forgiveness through your example?
8. When Peter talks about the Kingdom of God as Zion, which is Heaven and Earth coming together forever with the Second Coming of King Jesus, what things are you most looking forward to in Zion?

Pray it out: Ways for group members to pray together

1. What things that make your soul sick can we pray for and help you "put away" once and for all?
2. How can we join you in thanking God for ways He has allowed you to taste His goodness like a great meal?
3. Is there any area of your life that is not founded on Jesus Christ as the first priority and cornerstone that we can help you with by

starting with prayer?

4. What things can we help you "abstain from" because they "war against your soul" with prayer and loving support?
5. Who in your life does not know Jesus but knows you that we can be praying for that they see Jesus in you?
6. What good things is God teaching you, doing in you, and doing through you that we can thank God for?

WEEK 4: 1 PETER 2:13-25

Scripture:

[13]Be subject for the Lord's sake to every human institution,
whether it be to the emperor as supreme, [14]or to governors as sent
by him to punish those who do evil and to praise those who do
good. [15]For this is the will of God, that by doing good you should
put to silence the ignorance of foolish people. [16]Live as people who
are free, not using your freedom as a cover-up for evil, but living as
servants of God. [17]Honor everyone. Love the brotherhood. Fear God.
Honor the emperor. [18]Servants, be subject to your masters with all
respect, not only to the good and gentle but also to the unjust. [19]For
this is a gracious thing, when, mindful of God, one endures sorrows
while suffering unjustly. [20]For what credit is it if, when you sin and
are beaten for it, you endure? But if when you do good and suffer for
it you endure, this is a gracious thing in the sight of God. [21]For to this
you have been called, because Christ also suffered for you, leaving you
an example, so that you might follow in his steps. [22]He committed no
sin, neither was deceit found in his mouth. [23]When he was reviled, he
did not revile in return; when he suffered, he did not threaten, but
continued entrusting himself to him who judges justly. [24]He himself
bore our sins in his body on the tree, that we might die to sin and
live to righteousness. By his wounds you have been healed. [25]For you
were straying like sheep, but have now returned to the Shepherd and
Overseer of your souls.

Introduction and overview:

Seemingly everything in our life pulls us toward rebellion. We have a seed of rebellion from Adam that causes us to trend toward pride, rebellion, and defiance. Making matters worse, for those of us who live in America, our entire nation was the result of independence from authority – something that has both positive and negative implications. In the 60's and 70's, an entire counterculture arose based upon protests, sexual deviancy, drug and alcohol abuse, and self-expression as the highest good in place of honoring God. Today, we even expect teenagers to rebel against their parents as a rite of passage. The result is defiance, debt, destruction, and defiance across our entire culture. The countercultural emphasis of Peter's entire argument in this section is that God is our ultimate authority, and that God works through imperfect authorities in our lives and that a major part of Christian maturity is learning how to relate to authority.

Think it out: Questions for personal study

1. Based upon the big idea of verses 13-14, make a list of the authorities over you (e.g. parent, coach, pastor, politician, employer, teacher, etc.).
2. List the words that Peter uses to explain Christian living in verses 16-19 (e.g. free, servants, honor, love, fear, etc.).
3. How is a Christian's behavior at work, especially when mistreated, a great opportunity to show forth our Christian faith like in verses 18-21?
4. In addition to submitting to authority, list some occasions that godly civil disobedience is honored in Scripture (e.g. Hebrews in Exodus 1:17; Daniel and his friends in Daniel 1,3,6; Peter and the Apostles in Acts 5:27-29).
5. How did Jesus Christ both submit to the political authorities over Him, and also practice holy civil disobedience by not doing what was commanded when it was sinful?
6. How does Peter tie Jesus' suffering for us to our suffering for Him in verses 20-25?

Talk it out: Questions for group discussion

1. How does Jesus model for us submission to divine and human authority?
2. How does Jesus model for us submission to divine authority but civil disobedience to evil human authority that is demanding we violate God's authority?
3. Who is under your authority? How would they explain the way you treat them and exercise your authority?
4. Who is in authority over you? How would they explain the way you treat their authority?
5. Honestly, how do you relate to God's authority over every area of your life?
6. How have you suffered for your Christian faith? What comfort or encouragement do you find in Peter's words?

7. What does a world/nation/church/family/company look like if everyone rebels against every authority resulting in total anarchy?

Walk it out: Questions for personal action

1. Is there any authority over you that you have responded poorly to and need to apologize to?
2. Is there a change of attitude that you need to have toward someone in authority over you so that you can show the love of Christ to them?
3. Are there people under your authority that you need to apologize to and seek to treat better?
4. What good and evil examples of authority have you experienced in your life?
5. Are there ways that you have used, or are using, your freedom in Christ to say or do evil?
6. Why is God a better authority over your life than you are?
7. How have you suffered for doing good and for doing evil?
8. Do you really understand that your sinful rebellion causes Jesus the suffering of the cross as verses 21-25 say? What does Jesus' suffering for you reveal about His love for you?

Pray it out: Ways for group members to pray together

1. Which people in authority over you can we pray for? Which people under your authority can we pray for?
2. Which people in your past have hurt you and do you need to forgive so you can heal up and relate to authority figures in a healthier way?
3. Since Satan is the Father of rebellion, is there any area of your life not under God's authority that we can lovingly help you surrender, starting by praying for you to escape Satan's trap?
4. What does it mean to follow in Jesus' "example" of suffering so "that you might follow in his steps"?
5. How can we join you in thanking God for His authority over you that has let you "die to sin", "live to righteousness", and "healed" something broken in you?

WEEK 5: 1 PETER 3:1-7

Scripture:

[1]Likewise, wives, be subject to your own husbands, so that even
if some do not obey the word, they may be won without a word
by the conduct of their wives, [2]when they see your respectful and
pure conduct. [3]Do not let your adorning be external—the braiding of
hair and the putting on of gold jewelry, or the clothing you wear—
[4]but let your adorning be the hidden person of the heart with the
imperishable beauty of a gentle and quiet spirit, which in God's sight
is very precious. [5]For this is how the holy women who hoped in God
used to adorn themselves, by submitting to their own husbands, [6]as
Sarah obeyed Abraham, calling him lord. And you are her children, if
you do good and do not fear anything that is frightening. [7]Likewise,
husbands, live with your wives in an understanding way, showing
honor to the woman as the weaker vessel, since they are heirs with
you of the grace of life, so that your prayers may not be hindered.

Introduction and overview:

The Bible teaches that marriage was a sacred covenant created by God for one man and one woman to illustrate the loving relationship between Jesus Christ and the Church that He loves and serves like a husband loves and serves his wife. For this reason, a Christian marriage is part of worship of God, as well as being a witness to the world, as well as the world in which we raise our children to learn about God. Continuing the theme of humble, godly servant leadership that Peter began in the previous section, he speaks specifically to husbands and wives, including the difficult situation that some wives who have gotten saved after marrying experience when their husband has not yet met Jesus Christ.

Think it out: Questions for personal study

For Women

1. What is the difference between a wife and husband in a loving marriage honoring each other versus women in general deferring to men in general? How are Peter's words solely for marriage in specific and not a general rule for all men and

women in general?

2. Make a list of the words and concepts Peter uses to describe godly character for women (e.g. respectful, pure, character, self-control, inward beauty, etc.).
3. How are Abraham and Sarah far from perfect people, but hopeful examples that God can make a good marriage and family from two very dysfunctional people?
4. Why is it important for the health of the marriage and family for the husband to be the spiritual leader, loving and leading like Jesus, so that the wife and children are blessed?
5. How can a Christian woman who is married to a non-Christian man seek to bring him to Jesus in the most effective ways?
6. Unlike the culture, since God sees the heart, why does He place so much emphasis on prioritizing not just having a beautiful body, but more importantly a beautiful soul?

For Men

1. What does it mean in very practical ways to live in an understanding way with your wife that looks at things from her perspective and considers her needs above your own?
2. How are you doing at honoring your wife? How would she say you do not honor her?
3. What are the ways that a man can use the strength of his physical size, volume of his voice, or threat of his punishment to be domineering, overbearing, and abusive toward a woman?
4. Why is it important to consider your wife God's daughter and understand that her Father won't bless you if you don't bless her?
5. What happens to the prayers of a man who does not listen to and love his wife? Why is it fair for God the Father to treat a husband the way he treats his wife if he's being a bad husband?
6. How does Peter's commands to husbands not allow chauvinism to be the culture of the home and marriage that causes a woman to live in "fear" because the man is "frightening"?

Talk it out: Questions for group discussion

1. What is the best marriage you have ever seen? What made it great?

2. Women, who is the best example of a wife you have seen? Why?
3. Men, who is the best example of a husband you have seen? Why?
4. How is the example of Abraham and Sarah's messed up marriage and encouragement that God can make a great marriage and family through very flawed people helpful?
5. Women, how can a husband learn to better live with a wife in an understanding way?
6. Men, how can a wife understand the things that make her husband feel respected and disrespected?

Walk it out: Questions for personal action

For Women

1. If married, how can you ask your husband the ways he finds you respectful and disrespectful?
2. If you declare war on your husband, and have children, what example are you setting for the children in relation to both their parents?
3. What are the ways you have tried to change your husband that did not work? Have you honestly tried to influence them with Peter's principles over an extended period of time?
4. What does the Holy Spirit most convict you of as you read these Bible verses?
5. Do you want your sons to marry a woman just like you? If not, what needs to change?
6. If a woman treated your son the way you have treated your husband, how would you feel about them?
7. What do you need to apologize to your husband for, and ask him to forgive you for, so that healing can come to your marriage?

For Men

1. If married, how can you humbly ask your wife ways she feels honored/considered by you, as well as ways she feels dishonored/ignored by you?
2. If married, how can you humbly ask your wife if there is anything about you that causes her "fear", or that she or the children find "frightening"?

3. Have you made it your life assignment to be the expert student of your wife, knowing more about her and knowing her more than anyone else? If not, what needs to change?
4. What does the Holy Spirit most convict you of as you read these Bible verses?
5. Do you want your daughter to marry a man just like you? If not, what needs to change?
6. If a man treated your daughter the way you treat His daughter (your wife), how would you feel about them?
7. What do you need to apologize to your husband for, and ask him to forgive you for, so that healing can come to your marriage?

Pray it out: Ways for group members to pray together

(Break into male and female groups for prayer this week)

1. Are there any Christians you know who are married to non-Christians that you can be praying for?
2. How can the men in the group be praying for and encouraging each other to be better men and husbands?
3. How can the women in the group be praying for and encouraging each other to be better women and wives?
4. Are there any singles in the group you can be praying for to be godly and if married one day to have a holy, healthy, happy marriage?
5. For the married, on a scale of 1-10 (1 being we are in crisis, 10 being we are in the best marital season of our life), how would you score your marriage today? Make sure to pray for everyone's marriage to improve, and covenant to share your score with your spouse on the way home and discuss how to improve things without arguing, defending, or fighting but uniting, serving, and praying!

WEEK 6: 1 PETER 3:8-22

Scripture:

[8]Finally, all of you, have unity of mind, sympathy, brotherly love,
a tender heart, and a humble mind. [9]Do not repay evil for evil or
reviling for reviling, but on the contrary, bless, for to this you were
called, that you may obtain a blessing. [10]For "Whoever desires to love
life and see good days, let him keep his tongue from evil and his lips
from speaking deceit; [11]let him turn away from evil and do good; let
him seek peace and pursue it. [12]For the eyes of the Lord are on the
righteous, and his ears are open to their prayer. But the face of the
Lord is against those who do evil." [13]Now who is there to harm you
if you are zealous for what is good? [14]But even if you should suffer
for righteousness' sake, you will be blessed. Have no fear of them,
nor be troubled, [15]but in your hearts honor Christ the Lord as holy,
always being prepared to make a defense to anyone who asks you
for a reason for the hope that is in you; yet do it with gentleness and
respect, [16]having a good conscience, so that, when you are slandered,
those who revile your good behavior in Christ may be put to shame.
[17]For it is better to suffer for doing good, if that should be God's
will, than for doing evil. [18]For Christ also suffered once for sins, the
righteous for the unrighteous, that he might bring us to God, being
put to death in the flesh but made alive in the spirit, [19]in which he
went and proclaimed to the spirits in prison, [20]because they formerly
did not obey, when God's patience waited in the days of Noah, while
the ark was being prepared, in which a few, that is, eight persons,
were brought safely through water. [21]Baptism, which corresponds
to this, now saves you, not as a removal of dirt from the body but as
an appeal to God for a good conscience, through the resurrection of
Jesus Christ, [22]who has gone into heaven and is at the right hand of
God, with angels, authorities, and powers having been subjected to
him.

Introduction and overview:

When all is said and done, there will only be two cultures: Heaven, and Hell. Today, the choices we make every day either invite Heaven down into our lives, families, and churches, or pull hell up into our lives, families, and churches. In this section, Peter compares and contrasts these two cultures, urging and welcoming Christians to experience the culture of God's Kingdom right now so that life is marked by "unity...sympathy...love...a tender heart...a humble mind...a blessing...good...peace...gentleness...respect...good conscience..."

Think it out: Questions for personal study

1. Read 1 Peter 3:8-22 and make note of all the words and concepts that relate to the culture of Hell.
2. Read 1 Peter 3:8-22 and make note of all the words and concepts that relate to the culture of Heaven.
3. How is part of Christian living suffering for doing the right things sometimes like verses 13-17 say?
4. How does Peter connect living with character and earning the opportunity to earn the trust of non-Christians so that they ask us questions about Jesus like in verses 13-15?
5. How does baptism identify a Christian with the suffering, death, burial, and resurrection of Jesus according to 1 Peter 3:18-22 and Romans 6:1-11?

Talk it out: Questions for group discussion

1. Sometimes, Christians suffer for doing evil, and other times for doing good. How have you experienced both kinds of suffering in your life?
2. 1 Peter 3:10 quotes Psalm 34:12-16, an entire chapter on tasting and seeing the goodness of God. Have someone in the group read all of Psalm 34 aloud and see how the Holy Spirit uses that amazing chapter to build faith and hope in your group!
3. Who answered your questions about Jesus Christ and helped you become a Christian? How did their lifestyle help you trust them?
4. How is the response to evil that Peter teaches completely countercultural? Why is it important to respond to God rather than react to people when we are hurt or offended?
5. How is suffering a normal part of the Christian life on earth into we get Home into the Kingdom?
6. What does it mean, very practically, to "honor Christ the Lord" with every aspect of your life?

Walk it out: Questions for personal action

1. Are there any areas of your life where you are pulling the culture of hell up through such things as bitterness, vengeance, slander, etc.? What does it look like to forgive, heal up, move on, and not get stuck in that deathly cycle?
2. Do you want to "see good days" and "love life"? How does the lifestyle of 3:8-12 make that possible?
3. Which people have you met that invite the culture of Heaven down into their life and relationships? What can you learn from their example?
4. Who in your life is watching how you respond to tough times and what are they seeing?
5. What questions about Christ and Christianity do you need to study so that you can best answer people who have those questions?
6. How are you doing at saying what is true with "gentleness and respect" so that you are building people up instead of beating people up?
7. When Peter reminds us that God rescued Noah and his family from the flood, how does that apply to your life and trusting God to deliver you and your family?
8. How does seeing Jesus "at the right hand of God, with angels, authorities, and powers" now "subjected to him" inspire you to trust Him, pray to Him, and remain loyal to Him?

Pray it out: Ways for group members to pray together

1. Who has blessed you? Who do you need to bless like in 3:9?
2. What changes need to be made for you to "love life" and "see good days" like in 3:10?
3. Who do you need to forgive, give to Jesus, and not seek revenge against so that you can heal up and move on with your life?
4. Which non-Christians do you have opportunity to answer questions for that we can be praying for?
5. How does spiritual warfare often show up in your relationships, especially with your closest family and friends? How can we pray to invite the Holy Spirit and culture of Heaven into those relationships?

6. As God delivered Noah and his family, what are the ways we can thank God for delivering you and your family?

WEEK 7: 1 PETER 4:1-11

Scripture:

[1]Since therefore Christ suffered in the flesh, arm yourselves with the same way of thinking, for whoever has suffered in the flesh has ceased from sin, [2]so as to live for the rest of the time in the flesh no longer for human passions but for the will of God. [3]For the time that is past suffices for doing what the Gentiles want to do, living in sensuality, passions, drunkenness, orgies, drinking parties, and lawless idolatry. [4]With respect to this they are surprised when you do not join them in the same flood of debauchery, and they malign you; [5]but they will give account to him who is ready to judge the living and the dead. [6]For this is why the gospel was preached even to those who are dead, that though judged in the flesh the way people are, they might live in the spirit the way God does. [7]The end of all things is at hand; therefore be self-controlled and sober-minded for the sake of your prayers. [8]Above all, keep loving one another earnestly, since love covers a multitude of sins. [9]Show hospitality to one another without grumbling. [10]As each has received a gift, use it to serve one another, as good stewards of God's varied grace: [11]whoever speaks, as one who speaks oracles of God; whoever serves, as one who serves by the strength that God supplies—in order that in everything God may be glorified through Jesus Christ. To him belong glory and dominion forever and ever. Amen.

Introduction and overview:

There is an incredibly important concept in this section of Scripture for every Christian to learn in every area of their life. There is a massive difference between ownership, and "stewardship". Since God is the maker of everyone and everything, technically He is the owner of all. Since God entrusts some of what He owns for us to manage, we are His stewards who will give an account to Him for how we treated the people, things, and opportunities in this life that He entrusted to us. Our body our mind, our wealth, our relationships, our family, and our spiritual gifts are all from God and to be used by us in the ways that the Owner wants.

Think it out: Questions for personal study

1. How did Christ live as a steward of His life doing what the Father wanted and setting an example for Christians (verses 1-2)?
2. Once you become a Christian, why does God have the right to tell you what you can and cannot do with your body – especially in terms of things like food, drink, sex and the like (verse 3)?
3. Why do non-Christians not even understand the reason that Christians behave differently and that a new Christian has a deep change of lifestyle to make (verses 4-6)?
4. What is the list of things that God your owner commands for the stewardship of your life (verses 7-11)?
5. Which non-Christians do you need to invite into your home and life so they understand that God has also invited them into a relationship with them (verse 9)?
6. What gifts and abilities has God given you, and how can you use those for meaningful ministry starting in your local church (verses 10-11)?

Talk it out: Questions for group discussion

1. In your own words, how would you explain God as the owner of your life, and yourself as the steward?
2. What people and things has God given you to steward?
3. What changes happened in your life once you met Jesus? What motivated those changes?
4. How do non-Christian family and friends who see themselves as the owner of their life not even understand who you are or why you live the way you do?
5. What spiritual gifts and abilities has God given you to use for meaningful ministry? How does it feel in your soul when you do the things God has made you to do?

Walk it out: Questions for personal action

1. How does walking with Jesus require walking away from your old life (verses 1-6)?
2. Paul mentions living in "sin" in verse 1 versus living in the "spirit" in verse 6. Go through this section of Scripture and mark what fits in each category.
3. What does living "self-controlled" look like for you in very

specific areas and ways (verse 7)?

4. What people are hardest for you to "keep on loving...earnestly" (verse 8)? How can you get from God the Spirit the love you need to share with them?
5. What sins do you simply need to forgive, flush, and considered finished so you can "keep loving one another" (verse 8)?
6 . Whose love, in addition to Jesus, has covered your sins (verse 8)?
7. Which Christians first practiced hospitality to you and invited you into their life to see Jesus (verse 9)?
8. What are the various ways that Peter is teaching that the quality of our relationships truly reveals the sincerity of our Christian faith?

Pray it out: Ways for group members to pray together

1. Is there any area of your life that you need prayer and support to improve your stewardship in (e.g. physical health, financial generosity, service to others, etc.)?
2. What are the big changes that came in your life once God got a hold of you that you are most thankful for that we can praise God for?
3. Who has God put in your life that does not know Jesus but if you befriend them and do life with them, they might come to know Him?
4. Are there any areas in your life that the "grumbling" needs to simply stop?
5. What are the areas of ministry service that God has burdened you for that we can help pray into reality with you?

WEEK 8: 1 PETER 4:12-19

Scripture:

12Beloved, do not be surprised at the fiery trial when it comes
upon you to test you, as though something strange were happening
to you. 13But rejoice insofar as you share Christ's sufferings, that you
may also rejoice and be glad when his glory is revealed. 14If you are
insulted for the name of Christ, you are blessed, because the Spirit
of glory and of God rests upon you. 15But let none of you suffer as
a murderer or a thief or an evildoer or as a meddler. 16Yet if anyone
suffers as a Christian, let him not be ashamed, but let him glorify God
in that name. 17For it is time for judgment to begin at the household
of God; and if it begins with us, what will be the outcome for those
who do not obey the gospel of God? 18And "If the righteous is scarcely
saved, what will become of the ungodly and the sinner?" 19Therefore
let those who suffer according to God's will entrust their souls to a
faithful Creator while doing good.

Introduction and overview:

God the Father completely loved His Son, Jesus Christ. Looking at how Jesus was treated, and what Jesus endured during His life on the earth, it certainly did not look like He was loved by God. What Jesus endured was for the glory of God and good of others, at His own expense. Not only did Jesus suffer, but the Father and Spirit suffered with Him while watching the Person they loved the most suffer the most. What is true of Christ is true of Christians. We are "beloved" by God as Jesus is. We also "share Christ's sufferings" with "fiery trial" that feels like hell has been unleashed in our life. If we trust that God loves us, remember what Jesus endured for us, and invite the Spirit to empower us as He did Jesus, we can "rejoice and be glad", "not be ashamed", and "glorify God", as we "entrust...[our] souls to a faithful Creator" and persist in "doing good".

Think it out: Questions for personal study

1. Why is it so important to start everything with believing we are loved by God and "beloved" (verse 12)?
2. What fiery trials have you faced in your life that feel like hell was

unleashed (verse 12)?

3. Why is it oddly a good thing if we are treated like Jesus and suffer for doing what is right in the eyes of God (verses 13-16)?
4. How does God use fiery trials and tests to purify us by burning sin and folly out of our lives (verses 17-18)?
5. In verse 18, Peter quotes Proverbs 11:31. That chapter compares and contrasts a godly versus an ungodly lifestyle so read all of Proverbs 11 to get the heart of what Peter is communicating.
6. How is it an act of deep faith for a suffering Christian to keep trusting God and doing good (verse 19)?

Talk it out: Questions for group discussion

1. How does it feel to hear God call you "beloved"?
2. What fiery trials have felt like hell was unleashed in your life?
3. How is suffering for God part of our worshipping God?
4. How have you experienced the Holy Spirit coming in greater power to help you in seasons when you are under the most stress and struggle?
5. How has God used fiery trials and tests to purify your faith, burning sin and folly out of your life?
6. Who have you seen suffer trials that has responded so much like Jesus that it inspired you?

Walk it out: Questions for personal action

1. What is your current fiery trial (verse 12)?
2. When tough times come, do you act surprised or accept it as part of the Christian life (verse 12)?
3. How can you "rejoice and be glad" in your current life circumstances (verse 13)?
4. Why should a Christian expect some people to slander and insult them for standing with Jesus (verse 14)?
5. How have you suffered both for doing good and evil (verses 15-16)?
6. Why should we have higher expectations for Christian conduct than that of non-Christians (verses 17-18)?
7. How has God used suffering to increase your faith and love for God, bending even something bad for His glory and your good (verse 19)?

8. How has God proven Himself to be our "faithful Creator" (verse 19)?

Pray it out: Ways for group members to pray together

1. Do you have a current fiery trial that is testing your faith?
2. Are you currently suffering? If so, how? Is your suffering for righteousness, unrighteousness or a bit of both?
3. What things can you rejoice and be glad for in this season of your life?
4. How are you seeing the Holy Spirit rest on you in greater power to empower you through this season of life as the greater pressure you face brings the greater presence and power He gives?
5. How can we support you in prayer to entrust your soul to your faithful God?

WEEK 9: 1 PETER 5:1-14

Scripture:

[1]So I exhort the elders among you, as a fellow elder and a witness
of the sufferings of Christ, as well as a partaker in the glory that is
going to be revealed: [2]shepherd the flock of God that is among
you, exercising oversight, not under compulsion, but willingly,
as God would have you; not for shameful gain, but eagerly; [3]not
domineering over those in your charge, but being examples to the
flock. [4]And when the chief Shepherd appears, you will receive the
unfading crown of glory. [5]Likewise, you who are younger, be subject
to the elders. Clothe yourselves, all of you, with humility toward one
another, for "God opposes the proud but gives grace to the humble."
[6]Humble yourselves, therefore, under the mighty hand of God so
that at the proper time he may exalt you, [7]casting all your anxieties
on him, because he cares for you. [8]Be sober-minded; be watchful.
Your adversary the devil prowls around like a roaring lion, seeking
someone to devour. [9]Resist him, firm in your faith, knowing that the
same kinds of suffering are being experienced by your brotherhood
throughout the world. [10]And after you have suffered a little while, the
God of all grace, who has called you to his eternal glory in Christ, will
himself restore, confirm, strengthen, and establish you. [11]To him be the
dominion forever and ever. Amen. [12]By Silvanus, a faithful brother as I
regard him, I have written briefly to you, exhorting and declaring that
this is the true grace of God. Stand firm in it. [13]She who is at Babylon,
who is likewise chosen, sends you greetings, and so does Mark, my
son. [14]Greet one another with the kiss of love. Peace to all of you who
are in Christ.

Introduction and overview:

Some years ago, my youngest daughter told me that she had a desire in her heart to take a fun daddy/daughter trip with me to Alaska. Included in that desire was the longing to go see a real sled-dog team. So, we did exactly what my lovely little lady wanted to do and made memories that will last a lifetime. As we were with a sled dog team, the man who ran the team explained to us how a team rises or falls with the lead dog. A good lead dog makes the whole team succeed, a bad lead dog makes the whole team fail and can even cause injury or death. The stakes are very high. What is true of sled dog teams is true of all teams. For this reason, Peter ends his first letter to the members of Team Jesus in various local churches by reminding the senior leaders of the importance of their role in leading in love.

Think it out: Questions for personal study

1. Read John 21:15-17 where Jesus commissions Peter as a shepherd to feed the sheep as the backdrop for Peter's teaching on shepherding the flock of God in 1 Peter 5.
2. Make note of the things Peter says should not be part of Christ-like leadership.
3. Make a note of the things that Peter says should be part of Christ-like leadership.
4. In verses 12-13 Peter mentions by name the godly wonderful people he was grateful for. Who would be on your list?
5. What is the connection between pride and the demonic realm with Satan, who is the first leader to ever become proud, in verses 5-10?
6. List out the things God promises to faithful leaders in verse 10?
7. Peter ends by speaking of a special "peace" that only comes to those "who are in Christ". How have you experienced this peace?

Talk it out: Questions for group discussion

1. Who sees you as a spiritual leader (e.g. spouse, child, employee, etc.) and would benefit most from you learning these leadership lessons from Peter?
2. Which spiritual leader in your life has most exemplified the Christ-like character that Peter lists?
3. How is pride the leadership model of Satan and humility the leadership model of Jesus?
4. What are practical ways you can be "casting all your anxieties on him, because he cares for you"?
5. Peter mentions the people he is grateful for. Who would make your list and why?

Walk it out: Questions for personal action

1. Who do you shepherd, and who shepherds you (verses 1-4)?
2. Since Jesus is the "chief Shepherd", what are His values and culture that you need to be cultivating and creating (verse 4)?
3. What are some practical ways that when you clothe your body each morning you can also remember to clothe your soul in humility (verse 5)?
4. How big of a struggle are pride and anxiety for you (verses 6-7)?
5. What precisely does being "sober minded" and "watchful" regarding Satan's work in your life look like (verse 8)?
6. What does resisting Satan look like in practical areas of your life (e.g. temptation, unforgiveness, lies, etc.) (verse 9)?
7. After Satan has beat you up, how has God come to build you up just as He did Jesus following the temptation from Satan (verse 10)? (cf. Mathew 4:1-11 emphasis on verse 11).
8. Peter wrote a letter to lovingly encourage Christians. Who should you write a letter to for the same purpose?

Pray it out: Ways for group members to pray together

1. What are some specific ways that Jesus has been a Good Shepherd to you that we can thank God for?
2. What areas of your life can we pray for you to stand firm in the grace of God and not give up or give in?
3. Peter named people that he wanted to publicly encourage and thank. Who should you do that for?
4. Peter wrote a letter to love and encourage people he cared for. Who should we pray for you to do the same for?
5. After studying 1 Peter, if you had to summarize all you've learned in one word, what would that word be?
6. As we finish 1 Peter, what would your final takeaway, lesson learned, or life change experience be that we could join you in thanking God for?

CHAPTER 4

A 9-PART 1 PETER STUDY GUIDE FOR FAMILIES

Like newborn infants, long for the pure spiritual milk, that by it you may grow up into salvation— if indeed you have tasted that the Lord is good.

- 1 Peter 2:2-3

When our kids are little, we feed them milk. As they get older, we adjust their diet to encourage their health and growth.

What is true of our child's body is also true of their soul. When they are little, we pray over them, sing over them, and read the Word of God aloud over them so that our child grows up in God's presence. As our kids get a bit older, we read an age appropriate children's Bible to them until they are old enough to read it to us and encourage them to pray for themselves and others as they get older. Eventually, our kids get old enough that we can start to have more advanced conversations with them about the Lord, and they learn to express their own thoughts about God in their own words and ask us questions to help their learning.

Many of these types of conversations in our family over the years happened at our dinner table. Now that our children are all in their teens and twenties, we continue to have these kinds of conversations over dinner as year-after-year the discussions go deeper and deeper. Our goal as parents, and my goal as head of household leading us spiritually, was to not only feed our children's bodies, but also their hearts, minds, and souls like Jesus taught so they could be healthy in every way.

We want you to enjoy these same kinds of rich conversations and healthy relationships with your kids. The following is a series of practical tools to help you get started. To be clear, none of these are rules to be strictly followed, but merely tools to get you started. Sometimes, your kids won't feel like talking about deep things and just want to hang out – which is fine. Sometimes, your kids will have something else on their mind they want to discuss – which is fine. Sometimes, you will start a conversation and it will wander off course – which is fine. The goal is not to finish a curriculum but to build a happy, holy, and healthy family. This is the heart of what of Psalm 128:3–4, which says, "Your wife will be like a fruitful vine within your house; your children will be like olive shoots around your table. Behold, thus shall the man be blessed who fears the LORD."

Here's a few suggestions:

1. Regularly gather around the table for family dinner as a sacred routine that is a normal and fun part of life.
2. Turn technology off so that people can connect with each other.
3. Have a Bible on the table.
4. Have someone open the meal in prayer.
5. Start the meal by simply asking questions that get everyone talking. At our house this would include questions like:
   - "Is there anything anyone is thankful for this week"?
   - "Is there anyone or anything we can be praying for this week?"
   - "What do you feel like God is teaching you lately?"
   - "Is there anything you need or that we can help you with this week?"
   - "What was your highlight this week?"
   - "What was your one sermon takeaway from church?"
   - "Is there anything you are working on or excited about in the upcoming week?"
   - "Does anyone have a funny story to share from this week?"

   If any prayer opportunities arise, take a moment right then and there to pray for that praise or need. Some issues will arise that would be best discussed privately at another time without everyone involved and it is important if a family member raises that kind of issue that the parents follow up privately to love and serve the child.
6. As a dad, this is also a good time to thank and encourage family

members in front of one another so that they are built up by you and learn to build one another up. This can be thanking mom for something she did that week or encouraging the kids for something they did. The dad has a unique opportunity to set a culture of love, fun, respect, encouragement, and friendship among family members.

7. Ask the discussion questions written for each day's lesson. If your kids are older (i.e., junior high and up), you might consider using the Life Groups questions if they are better suited for your children. Lastly, parents need to let the conversation happen naturally. Listen carefully to the kids, let them answer the questions, and fill in whatever they miss or lovingly and gently explain whatever is helpful so that a pattern of trust is built encouraging the kids to bring their questions and needs to the parents in the context of a loving, fun, healthy, safe, godly relationship. If your kids don't know the answer, explain it to them, and then ask them to explain it in their own words.

WEEK 1: 1 PETER 1:1-12

Sunday
Bible Reading: 1 Peter 1:1–2
Word of the Day: Peter

Peter is the author of 1 and 2 Peter and so today the focus of the dinner discussion is helping your children learn about Peter. You can learn about more in chapter 1 of the study guide to refresh your memory. You can begin by asking them the following Bible questions:

1. Who was Peter?

The following are examples of things the kids might want to explain or discuss:

   a. He was the disciple Andrew's brother.
   b. He was a fisherman.
   c. He was married.
   d. He was Jewish.

2. What do you know about Peter's life?
   a. He became a disciple of Jesus so that Jesus was his teacher and the disciples were like a class in school.
   b. He spent three years with Jesus as a really close friend.

c. Jesus made him the leader of the disciples, like the Senior Pastor.
d. He wrote two books of the Bible (1 and 2 Peter).
e. He was a pastor who loved people.
f. He was crucified upside down for being a Christian.

Monday
Bible Reading: 1 Peter 1:1–2
Word of the Day: Jesus Christ

Peter begins his letter by speaking of Jesus Christ. So, today the focus is on who Jesus is and what he has done by discussing the following Bible questions:

1. Where was Jesus born? Bethlehem.
2. Where did Jesus grow up? Nazareth.
3. Who was Jesus' mommy? Mary.
4. Who was Jesus' adoptive daddy? Joseph.
5. Did Jesus have brothers and sisters? Yes.
6. Who were Jesus' half-brothers? James and Jude.
7. Is Jesus God? Yes.
8. Did Jesus ever sin? No.
9. Did Jesus ever marry or have kids? No.
10. Did Jesus love and play with kids? Yes.
11. How did Jesus die? Crucifixion.
12. Why did Jesus die? For our sins.
13. What happened to Jesus three days after he died? He resurrected and was alive forever.
14. How did Peter know Jesus? They were friends, Peter was Jesus' disciple or student, and for three years he was with Jesus to see His miracles, hear His preaching, and be with Him after He rose from death.
15. Where is Jesus today? In Heaven.
16. Do you know anyone else who was adopted like Jesus?
17. What do you think Jesus was like a kid?
18. Do you have any questions about Jesus?

Tuesday
Bible Reading: 1 Peter 1:1–2
Word of the Day: Trinity

Peter speaks of God the Father, God the Son Jesus Christ, and God the Holy Spirit. Christians call this the Trinity. Kind of like a mommy and daddy who are two people, but married and live together as one, there is one God in three persons (Father, Son, Spirit). The God of the Bible is a lot like a loving family and shows us how to be a loving family.

1. How many gods are there? There is One God.
2. What does Trinity mean? One God in three persons.
3. Who are the three members of the Trinity? Father, Son, and Holy Spirit.
4. Does the Bible use the word "trinity"? No, it is a word that Christians use to explain what the Bible teaches. The Bible also does not use the Word Bible and Christians use some words to explain what the Scriptures teach.
5. How is God a person? Examples include things like - God loves, laughs, thinks, feels, talks, has friends, etc.
6. Does God have a body? No, only Jesus had a body when He came to earth, but God the Father and God the Holy Spirit do not have bodies.
7. Are God the Father, Jesus Christ, and the Holy Spirit equally God? Yes, they have all the same "attributes", such as knowing everything, having all power, and being the Creator of the world and people.
8. Do other religions believe in the Trinity? No, only Christians believe in the Trinity.

Wednesday
Bible Reading: 1 Peter 1:1–2
Word of the Day: Grace

1 Peter 1:2 speaks of God's grace. The word grace is one of the most important words in the Bible because it tells us how God acts toward us. Grace means that God's love is seen in all the kind things he does for us. Simply, grace is getting good things we do not deserve. God gives grace to everyone, as evidenced by the fact that they are alive, can eat food, and can have fun. God gives extra grace to Christians by giving them Jesus so that their sins are forgiven, and God is their helpful friend. The following Bible questions can help start a discussion with your children about God's grace in their lives:

1. What is God's grace? Good things we do not deserve.
2. Why does God give grace? Because he is loving and good.
3. What has God given you in grace? Examples include life, health, a family, friends, fun, favorite possessions, pet, etc.
4. How have people given you grace? Examples include love, forgiveness, friendship, gifts, teaching, parents, church, etc.
5. What are some ways you can give grace to someone? Examples include loving them, serving them, praying for them, giving a present to them, etc.
6. Do other religions believe in God's grace? No, other religions say you have to work hard to get God to be nice to you. Only the Bible teaches that God is good and takes care of us out of his grace.
7. Who are some people that come to mind when you think of grace in terms of being generous and kind to you?

Thursday
Bible Reading: 1 Peter 1:3–9
Word of the Day: Cross

In this week's reading of 1 Peter 1:3–9, Peter focuses on the fact that Jesus died for our sins and conquered sin and death through his resurrection. So, this week we will focus on Jesus Christ's resurrection from death and examine a different reason each day why we believe in Jesus' resurrection. Today we will look at the facts surrounding Jesus' death and burial by discussing the following questions:

1. What is a cross? It is where they would kill people in the days of Jesus by nailing them through the hands and feet.
2. Why was Jesus crucified? He did not ever sin, but he died in our place for our sins so that we could be forgiven.
3. Did people know Jesus was going to die and resurrect? Yes, seven hundred years before Jesus was even born, God promised in Isaiah 53:8–12 that Jesus would die and rise. Jesus also promised that he would be crucified, die, and then resurrect in Matthew 12:38–40; Mark 8:31; 9:31; 10:33–34; and John 2:18–22. (You can look up and read these verses so that the children get an example of God's foreknowledge, which we discussed the previous week.)
4. Did Jesus really die on the cross? Yes. Prior to his crucifixion, Jesus had not slept all night, was beaten, and then was scourged, which killed many men in and of itself. Then he was crucified with

nails in his hands and feet. He was declared dead by an executioner, and a spear was run through his side, which pierced his heart. He was buried like a mummy in upwards of a hundred pounds of linens and spices, and then placed in a cold tomb cut out of rock without medical attention, food, or water. So, Jesus really did die on the cross.

5. Was Jesus' tomb easy to find? Yes. Jesus was poor and did not own a tomb because he could not afford one. So, after he died, a powerful and rich man named Joseph of Arimathea let Jesus be buried in his personal tomb in fulfillment of the prophecy of Isaiah 53:9, which promised Jesus would be buried "with a rich man in his death." A large stone was rolled over the tomb to ensure the body of Jesus was not stolen, the government's seal was placed on the stone to keep people out, and soldiers were placed on duty to guard Jesus' tomb. So, lots of people knew where Jesus was buried.
6. Do you believe that Jesus died on the cross? Why or why not?
7. How much does Jesus love you to go through all of this so He could be with you forever in Heaven?

Friday
Bible Reading: 1 Peter 1:10–12
Word of the Day: Prophets

In 1 Peter 1:10–12 Peter speaks about the Old Testament prophets. Prophets were people who spoke for God by preaching and/or writing what God told them. Prophets often predicted the future, letting people know what would happen before it actually did.

1. What is a prophet? A person in the Bible who preached and/or wrote for God.
2. How did someone become a prophet? God chose them to be a prophet.
3. Does God know the future? Yes, He knows the future and He controls it.
4. Did the prophets ever prophesy something that did not come true? No, the Bible teaches that a true prophet of God does not lie and they always tell the truth (Deut. 18:21–22).
5. Do any other religions have prophecy like Christianity? No, other religions do not have prophets who tell the future like Christianity

because their prophets are false prophets who do not work for God.

Saturday
Bible Reading: 1 Peter 1:10–12
Word of the Day: Prophecy
1 Peter 1:10–12 speaks of prophets who prophesy about Jesus in the Old Testament. These prophecies are very specific and were given hundreds of years before Jesus was even born. These prophecies reveal to us that God knows and controls the future, and that the Bible is true. Therefore, we will learn some specific Old Testament prophecies about Jesus, and it might be good for each family member to take turns reading the prophecies and telling what it predicted about Jesus Christ.

Isaiah 7:14 (700 BC): "'Therefore the Lord himself will give you a sign. Behold, the virgin shall conceive and bear a son, and shall call his name Immanuel'"

Micah 5:2 (700 BC): "But you, O Bethlehem Ephrathah, who are too little to be among the clans of Judah, from you shall come forth for me one who is to be ruler in Israel, whose origin is from of old, from ancient days [eternity]."

Malachi 3:1 (400 BC): "Behold, I send my messenger, and he will prepare the way before me. And the Lord whom you seek will suddenly come to his temple; and the messenger of the covenant in whom you delight, behold, he is coming, says the LORD of hosts". (It is important because the temple was destroyed in AD 70 and no longer exists; subsequently, the prophecy could not have been fulfilled anytime after AD 70.)

Zechariah 11:12-13 (500 BC): "Then I said to them, 'If it seems good to you, give me my wages; but if not, keep them.' And they weighed out as my wages thirty pieces of silver. Then the LORD said to me, 'row it to the potter'—the lordly price at which I was priced by them. So I took the thirty pieces of silver and threw them into the house of the LORD, to the potter"

Isaiah 53:1-11 (700 BC): "Yet it was the will of the LORD to crush him; he has put him to grief; when his soul makes an offering for sin, he shall see his o spring; he shall prolong his days; the will of the LORD shall prosper in his hand. Out of the anguish of his soul he shall see and be satisfied; by his knowledge shall the righteous one, my servant, make many to be accounted righteous, and he shall bear their iniquities"

WEEK 2: 1 PETER 1:13-25

Sunday
Bible Reading: 1 Peter 1:13–21
Word of the Day: Mind
Peter tells us to prepare our minds so that we can think like God wants us to, which helps us to live our life like God wants us to.

1. What things help you learn about God and how he wants you to think and live?
2. How does prayer to God help you learn about God?
3. How does reading the Bible help you learn about God?
4. How does going to church help you learn about God?
5. Why do we talk about God as a family?
6. What things have you learned about God lately?
7. If you could ask Jesus one question, what would you ask?

Monday
Bible Reading: 1 Peter 1:13–21
Word of the Day: Father
Peter teaches us that God is a father. Christians are like God's kids who are adopted into his family to be loved, taught, and cared for by him.

1. What does it mean that God is a Father, or a perfect Daddy?
2. What does it mean that when we become Christians it's like getting adopted into God's family the church?
3. Do you know anyone who was adopted?
4. Did Joseph adopt Jesus? Yes.
5. What does it mean that other Christians are like brothers and sisters?
6. Who are the Christians you know that feel like they are part of your family?

Tuesday
Bible Reading: 1 Peter 1:13–21

Word of the Day: Obedient

Peter says that Christians are supposed to be like obedient children. This means that we are supposed to obey God our Father like a good child obeys his or her parent.

1. Why do God and parents ask children to do good things and not do bad things? Because they love the children and want the best for them.
2. What does it mean to obey? It means that because of the love in your heart, you do what your parents and God ask of you.
3. What happens to children who do not obey God and their parents? They get into sin and their life is ruined.
4. Can you think of any times in your life when you did not obey God and your parents and something bad happened?
5. Are there any rules from the Bible or your home that you don't think are fair or right? Why?
6. Which rules from God or your parents are most difficult for you to obey? Why?
7. Parents, this is a good opportunity to demonstrate how God is a good gracious Father to you. Take a few moments and explain to your child a time in your life when you did not obey your parents or when you did not obey God and you suffered for it so that they learn that you both need God's help. Invite them to ask you any questions they may have about what you share.

Wednesday
Bible Reading: 1 Peter 1:13–21
Word of the Day: Holy

Peter tells us that God is holy and that Christians are to be holy. The Bible says God is holy more often than it mentions any of his other attributes, which means that holiness is very important. The word holy means "to be set apart". So, to be holy is to be different in a good way. As Christians, we do some things differently than other people because God loves us, we love God, and we want to be holy.

1. What does holiness mean? To be "set apart" or different in a good way compared to what some other people say and do.
2. What is the opposite of holiness? Unholiness or sin where we disobey God.
3. What are some things that Christians do that are different than

other people? Examples include believing Jesus is God, reading the Bible, praying, worshiping God, going to church, confessing our sins to God, and not doing bad sinful things like swearing at people, hitting people, or taking things that are not ours.
4. Have you ever had someone make fun of you for being holy and not sinning? Explain what happened and how you felt.
5. When you think of someone who is holy, who comes to mind?

Thursday
Bible Reading: 1 Peter 1:22–25
Word of the Day: Truth

Peter says that we should obey the truth. It is very important to know that God tells the truth. Truth is what is real and not a lie.

1. What is truth? Truth is what is real and from God.
2. What is the opposite of truth? Lies are the opposite of truth.
3. Where do we learn the truth? In the Bible.
4. Who always told the truth? Jesus always told the truth. Jesus says, "I tell you the truth" more than fifty times in the Gospel of John alone.
5. Who tells lies? Satan tells lies and Jesus says he is the father of lies in John 8:44.
6. Should we lie or tell the truth? Tell the truth like Jesus did.
7. What should we do when we lie? We should apologize to God and whomever we lied to because lying is a sin.

Friday
Bible Reading: 1 Peter 1:22–25
Word of the Day: Love

Peter says that Christians are to love God and one another. Love is one of the most important teachings in all of Christianity. Love comes from God because God is perfect love. When we love we are doing what God wants us to do.

1. Where does love come from? Love comes from God because God is love (1 John 4:8).
2. If God gives you love to share with other people, can you ever run out of love?
3. Who has loved you the most besides God?
4. What are the most loving things people have done for you?

5. What are some things you can do to love people?

Saturday
Bible Reading: 1 Peter 1:22–25
Word of the Day: Word of God

Peter says that we become Christians by hearing and believing the Word of God. The title "Word of God" refers to the Bible. This is because the Bible is the literal words of God and the perfect way that God speaks to us.

1. What is the Word of God? The Bible is the Word of God.
2. How many books are in the Bible? Sixty-six books.
3. How many books are in the Old Testament? Forty-nine books.
4 How many books are in the New Testament? Twenty-seven books.
5. How does God speak to us? Through the Bible.
6. What are your favorite lessons from the Bible or Bible stories?

WEEK 3: 1 PETER 2:1-12

Sunday
Bible Reading: 1 Peter 2:1-3
Word of the Day: Repentance

Peter says that we should put our sin away from us because it is bad. The word repentance is often used in the Bible to explain how we put our sins away from us. Repentance is very important because it shows us that when we do sin, we can ask Jesus to forgive us and he will help us to turn around and walk away from sin and be close to God. When we are doing something bad, God wants us to have Him help us change and start doing what is right.

1. What should we do when we sin? We should repent of our sin.
2. What is repentance? Telling God and whomever we sinned against we are sorry, asking their forgiveness, and letting God help us to stop sinning and do the right thing.
3. When was a time that someone did something bad, and they said they were sorry and changed? How did that make you feel?
4. Parents, this would be a good opportunity for you to speak from the example of your own life in an appropriate way. Tell your children some sin you wrestled with and how Jesus helped you to

repent of it and put it away. Invite your child to ask you any questions they may have about your repentance.

Monday
Bible Reading: 1 Peter 2:1-3
Word of the Day: Born again

Peter says that Christians are people who have been born again. What he means is that when we are born, we are physically alive but spiritually dead in that we don't love Jesus for being our God. However, when we become Christians, we are born a second time so that we are both physically alive and spiritually alive to God.

1. Parents, take a few minutes and explain to your children what they were like when they were a baby. Tell the funny stories and describe how much you loved them. Ask them if they have any questions about what they were like as babies. You may also want to show them some of their baby photos.
2. What do babies like to eat when they were born? Babies eat a lot of milk.
3. What are new Christians hungry for when they first become Christians and are born again? Peter says they are hungry for the Bible and like to learn about God from the Bible just like babies are hungry for milk.
4. Parents, explain to your children what new appetites for God and Scripture that you experienced when you became a Christian and were born again. Invite them to ask any questions they may have about changes in your life since you were born again as a Christian.

Tuesday
Bible Reading: 1 Peter 2:4-12
Word of the Day: Priesthood

Peter says that Christians are a priesthood. In the Old Testament the priests were God's people who served God in ministry. In the New Testament, Peter says that all Christians are priests, which means that we can have a direct relationship with God through Jesus Christ, and that our whole life is ministry for God.

1. Who were the priests in the Old Testament? They were like pastors who did ministry for God, taught the Bible, prayed, and

helped people.
2. Who are the priests in the New Testament? All Christians are called priests in the New Testament.
3. What are the ministries of people in your family? Examples include helping out parents, serving kids in school, looking after siblings, etc. Talk this point through with your children at length and help them to see how they have opportunities to do ministry and help people. Also share as parents what your ministries are.

Wednesday
Bible Reading: 1 Peter 2:4-12
Word of the Day: Cornerstone

Peter says that Jesus is our cornerstone. In Jesus' day many buildings were made out of stones cut out of rock, kind of like bricks. When a building was made, the very first stone that was laid on the bottom of the building was called the cornerstone. The cornerstone was the most important stone because it held up the entire building. So, when Peter says that Jesus is our cornerstone, he is saying that Jesus should be first in our life and everything in our life needs to be built on him. Think of it like playing with Legos or stacking blocks. The big piece you lay down to build everything on is your cornerstone.

1. What things do you like to build? How do you start building something (e.g. Legos, a blanket fort, stacked blocks, card house, etc.)?
2. What is a cornerstone? It is the first and most important stone that is laid down to make a building.
3. What does it mean that Jesus is our cornerstone? It means he is the most important Person in our life and that our whole life should be built on Him.
4. What happens to a building that has a bad cornerstone? The entire building breaks and falls to the ground.
5. What happens to someone's life if Jesus is not the cornerstone? Their life is not built for God and it falls apart, like a bad building.
6. If Jesus is the cornerstone, who are the other stones in God's building, the church? God's people are the other stones stacked together as the church.
7. You may want to go out and briefly show the kids the foundation of their home and explain how it holds everything up.

If the foundation was bad, everything would fall down. This is a good illustration for what Jesus does.

Thursday
Bible Reading: 1 Peter 2:4-12
Word of the Day: Stumbling stone

Everyone has tripped over a rock and fallen down. Peter says that, sadly, for some people, Jesus is like a rock that they trip and fall over. What he means is that some people do not believe Jesus is God or that he rose from death and so they are not Christians who love Jesus. Peter says that they trip over Jesus because they are don't like Jesus saying He is God and that people need His help.

1. When was a time that you tripped and fell?
2. Parents, explain the ways you have stumbled over Jesus but God picked you up to help you be a Christian.
3. For the child, is there anything about Jesus or Christianity that is hard for you to believe?
4. What does it mean that Jesus is a stumbling stone for non-Christians? It means that they do not love Jesus as God or think they need His help for their life.
5. What would you tell people who have questions about or problems with Jesus?
6. Do you know any non-Christians whom we should pray for and love in hopes that they become Christians?
7. Parents, take some time as a family to regularly pray for non-Christian family, friends, neighbors, etc., to become Christians.

Friday
Bible Reading: 1 Peter 2:4-12
Word of the Day: God's people

Peter says that Christians are God's people. What he means is that Christians believe in Jesus and live together as the church, kind of like a big family that loves and serves one another, or a team that works together.

1. What does it mean that we are God's people? It means that all Christians belong to God and are like a family or a team.
2. How many of God's people can you name that you know personally?

3. What are the benefits of being God's people? Examples include that our sins are forgiven, the Holy Spirit lives in us to help us, we get to pray to God, we get to have Christian friends and be involved in church, we can be together forever in Heaven, etc.
4. What do you like best about being one of God's people?
5. Parents, explain why you like being among God's people and how that has benefited you and your family.

Saturday
Bible Reading: 1 Peter 2:4-12
Word of the Day: Darkness and light
Sometimes word pictures are the best way to understand something. Peter uses the word picture of darkness and light to explain life with Jesus. He says that life without Jesus is like living in the dark and that life with Jesus is like living in the light.

1. What do you think about the dark? Examples include that it is scary, lonely, and bad.
2. What does Peter mean that living without Jesus is like living in the dark? Examples include that you are lonely, scared, and don't know God.
3. What do you think about warm sunlight? Examples include that it is fun, feels good, and makes you feel alive and happy.
4. What does Peter mean when he says that living with Jesus is like living in the light? Examples include that you are living and growing, happier, and not scared or lonely.
5. Do you ever get scared going to bed in the darkness? Explain. Parents, make sure to pray for your kids at bedtime and teach them to pray to Jesus themselves whenever they are scared at nighttime.
6. What are your favorite things to do on a warm sunny day?

WEEK 4: 1 PETER 2:13-25

Sunday
Bible Reading: 1 Peter 2:13–17
Word of the Day: Submission
God is in charge of everyone and everything because He is in ultimate authority. God also puts people in authority over us to help us learn

and grow. As long as the people in authority over us are not telling us to do something sinful against God, we are supposed to submit to them and do what they ask us.

1. Who is in ultimate authority and in charge of everyone and everything? God.
2. What human authorities has God put in authority over you? Examples include parents, teachers, coaches, Sunday school teachers, police, etc.
3. Should you submit to someone who tells you to sin? No.
4. Should you submit to people in authority who tell you to do good things? Yes.
5. What are some ways you have submitted to godly authority?
6. Parents, it is good to explain to your children that you are submissive to godly authority as well. Take some time explaining how you have to obey God, the government, police, your boss, doctor, church leaders, etc.

Monday
Bible Reading: 1 Peter 2:13–17
Word of the Day: Servants

Peter says that Christians are supposed to be servants. This is because Jesus is a servant (e.g., Mark 10:42–45; Phil. 2:5–11) who has served us by coming to earth, living without sin, dying for our sins, and rising for our salvation. Jesus did all of this out of humility and love even though He was God. Since Jesus has been so good to us, we want to follow His example and humbly serve others in love.

1. How is Jesus the greatest servant who has ever lived? Jesus is God and was humble enough to come to earth to serve people. Jesus has served more people than anyone who has ever lived and died for our sins, which is the greatest act of service anyone has ever done.
2. Who has served you and how have they served you?
3. Who in the family can you thank for serving this week?
4. Why do we serve people? Because Jesus has served us and we want to share God's love with other people.
5. Who does God want you to serve and how does he want you to serve them?

Tuesday
Bible Reading: 1 Peter 2:13–17
Word of the Day: Honor

Peter says that Christians are supposed to honor everyone. This does not mean that we agree with everyone, or that we like what everyone is doing. However, it does mean that we treat people with respect and love because that is how God treats people.

1. What does it mean to honor people? Examples include that we treat people with love and respect even if we disagree with them.
2. Can you remember a time when someone did not honor or respect you (e.g., called you a name or was mean) and how you felt?
3. Is there anyone you need to do a better job of honoring? How can you do that?
4. Is there anything that I/we (the parents) do or say that you don't think is honoring? Parents, this is a good time for you to examine your own life and parenting to see if you have been disrespectful to your children by being harsh, mean, or curt. If so, apologize to them, ask their forgiveness, and pledge to them and God that you will repent and grow in that area to do a better job of honoring them and setting a good example.

Wednesday
Bible Reading: 1 Peter 2:13–17
Word of the Day: Love

Peter says that Christians are supposed to love one another. This is because God is loving and wants us to treat one another the way he treats us. To help us love our Christian friends and church, God gives Christians the Holy Spirit who gives us love to share with others (Rom. 5:5). Love is doing what is best for other people.

1. Where does love come from? Love comes from God.
2. How has Jesus loved us? Examples include that he came into history as a person although he is God, lived without sin, died for our sins, rose for our salvation, sent the Holy Spirit to change us from the inside out, and is preparing a place for us right now in heaven.
3. What does it mean that Christians are supposed to love one another?

4. Which Christians have loved you well? How did they love you?
5. Whom have you loved well? How did you love them?
6. Is there anyone you need to love better and, if so, how can you do that?

Thursday
Bible Reading: 1 Peter 2:18–25
Word of the Day: Sorrow

Peter tells us that some things in life will give us sorrows or make us sad. This is because sometimes life is difficult. In hard times it is okay to be sad and even to cry. After all, even Jesus was sometimes sad and Isaiah 53:3 calls him "a man of sorrows." The shortest verse in the Bible says, "Jesus wept" (John 11:35). So, Christians are allowed to be honest about their feelings like Jesus was, which means sometimes we have joy and sometimes we have sorrow. When we have sorrow, God wants us to keep going and not give up but keep doing what is right.

1. What are some times in the Bible when Jesus had sorrow? Examples include Jesus' sadness that his friend Lazarus had died, when he prayed in the Garden of Gethsemane the night before he died, and when he saw his mother Mary at the foot of his cross.
2. What does the shortest verse in the Bible say? John 11:35 says, "Jesus wept."
3. Is it okay for Christians to sometimes be happy and sometimes be sad? Yes.
4. What are your happiest memories?
5. What are your saddest memories?
6. What are some things that you want to quit doing because they are difficult or make you sad? (e.g., schoolwork, chores)
7. Parents, this is a good opportunity to share with your children struggles in your life that are difficult for you to endure (e.g., illness, unemployment, financial shortfalls, a tough job). Explain to them what you are doing to endure and persevere and why.
8. How can we be praying for each other to endure things that are hard, or make us sad? Parents, this is a good time to take a few moments over dinner and pray for each other in areas needing endurance.

Friday
Bible Reading: 1 Peter 2:18–25
Word of the Day: Healing

Peter quotes Isaiah 53:5 and says that we can be healed because of Jesus' death on the cross. This means that in this life some people are healed of sickness. It also means that all Christians are healed after they die and resurrect with new bodies that never get sick or hurt ever again.

1. What does healing mean? It means that God heals our sickness by a miracle.
2. Does God want us to pray for sick people to be healed? Yes. (e.g., James 5:14)
3. Are there any sick people we should be praying for? Parents, this is a good opportunity to take some time and pray with your children for sick people your family knows.
4. Is every Christian healed in this life? No.
5. Is every Christian healed in heaven? Yes.
6. What do you think it will be like in heaven where no one gets sick, hurt, or dies?

Saturday
Bible Reading: 1 Peter 2:18–25
Word of the Day: Sheep

Peter says that people who sin are like straying sheep. Sheep are mentioned more than any other animal in the Bible, roughly 400 times altogether. Sheep often wander away from their shepherd who looks after them. This is dangerous because sheep do not have any way to defend themselves and wolves and other animals will kill them. When we sin and wander away from God, we are like sheep who are in danger of being hurt.

1. What kinds of animals are your favorite?
2. Which animal is mentioned the most in the Bible? Sheep.
3. How are people like sheep? We need to stay close to God for protection and if we wander away from God we are in danger like sheep.
4. Are sheep a strong and tough animal? No, they are nice but cannot fight back if other animals like wolves try to hurt them.
5. In what ways do you wander from God like sheep wander from

their shepherd?
6. Who looks after the sheep? The shepherd.
7. How are a mom or dad like a shepherd? They feed us, protect us, and love us.
8. How is Jesus our Shepherd?

WEEK 5: 1 PETER 3:1-7

Sunday
Bible Reading: 1 Peter 3:1–7
Word of the Day: Marriage
God is the one who made us male and female and invented marriage for one man and one woman (Gen. 2:18–25). The Bible also teaches that Jesus is like a husband and the church is like his wife whom he loves (Eph. 5:22–33). This means that Christians who get married are supposed to love one another like Jesus and the church. Peter was a pastor who wrote the letter that became a book of the Bible to help his people. Some of the women in his church were Christians who were married to men who were not Christians. The Bible teaches that Christians are only supposed to marry Christians (2 Cor. 6:14–15). But some Christians sin and marry non-Christians. Also, sometimes two non-Christians marry and then one of them becomes a Christian. It is very difficult for a Christian to be married to a non-Christian because they do not worship God together, pray together, study the Bible together, or want to do everything that God says.

1. Who is supposed to get married? One man and one woman.
2. Who invented marriage? God did.
3. Who were the first people to ever get married? Adam and Eve.
4. Should a Christian marry a non-Christian? No.
5. What are some ways it is difficult for a Christian to be married to a non-Christian? Examples include they do not worship God together, study the Bible together, or go to church together, and they will want to raise their children differently.
6. Parents, this is a good time for you to explain why you want your children to be Christians who only date and marry Christians. Answer any questions they may have about this important subject.
7. Parents, this is a good opportunity to answer any questions your

children may have about marriage. Explain your own marriage and how you met one another and courted (if you are married). Also explain to them the importance of being a Christian and marrying a Christian and why and how you will help decide whom they date and marry.

Monday
Bible Reading: 1 Peter 3:1–6
Word of the Day: Good deeds

Peter says that Christian women should be known for their good deeds and conduct. This is also true for every Christian. Just like God loves and serves us, we should love and serve others.

1. What are good deeds? Good things we do out of love for God and other people.
2. What are some good deeds a loving husband and wife do for each other?
3. Why is it good to start serving other people when you are little to help you get ready to be married one day?
4. Parents, this is a good opportunity for everyone in the family to give some examples of good deeds they have seen in the actions of other family members so as to encourage good deeds in one another.

Tuesday
Bible Reading: 1 Peter 3:1–6
Word of the Day: True beauty

Peter says that Christian women should dress with modesty. This does not mean that they should not dress attractively and nicely, but rather that they should not dress in a way that is not appropriate. Too often girls and women are pressured to be only concerned about what they look like on the outside rather than the inside. However, since God looks at our hearts, we should look at people's hearts also and see that their true beauty is their love for God and holy character.

1. What is true beauty? True beauty is what is in the heart of someone who loves God and other people.
2. Why is it important to have a beautiful heart that loves people, and beautiful soul that loves God?
3. How much pressure do you feel from media and friends to

dress a certain way and look a certain way?
4. When you think of someone who has beautiful character that loves God and people well, who do you think of?
5. Name one godly woman at a time from the Bible, tell what you know about her story, and share what good things we can learn from her life.

Wednesday
Bible Reading: 1 Peter 3:7
Word of the Day: Love

Peter says that Christian husbands are to be loving, kind, tender, and sweet to their wives. This is because marriage is a picture of Jesus' relationship with the church and husbands are to love their wives like Jesus loves the church. Love includes the words we say, the gifts we give, the time we spend together, how we serve, and how we touch one another. A husband is supposed to be a really good friend to his wife.

1. Why does Peter say that husbands must love their wives? Because husbands are to act like Jesus.
2. How can our words be loving? How can our words be unloving?
3. How can our service be loving? How can our service be unloving (e.g., we only serve people who serve us)?
4. How can our gifts be loving? How can our gifts be unloving?
5. How can our time together with people be loving? How can we be unloving when we spend time with people?
6. How can the way we touch people be loving (e.g., hugs)? How can we touch people in a way that is unloving (e.g., shoving, hitting)?

Thursday
Bible Reading: 1 Peter 3:7
Word of the Day: Weaker

Peter says that when someone is stronger than another person it is a sin for the stronger person to bully and push around the weaker person. Sometimes men sin terribly by pushing around and bullying their wives and children just because they are not as strong and tough.

1. How should we treat someone who is weaker (e.g., younger

children)? We should love and protect them and not push them around or bully them.
2. Is it a bad thing to be weaker than someone else? No, everyone is weaker than someone else.
3. What kinds of things do bullies do? Examples include they call names, they hurt people's feelings, they push or hit others, they make people do what they do not want to do, etc.
4. Is there anyone that you sometimes bully? If so, explain.
5. Is there anyone who sometimes bullies you? If so, explain.

Friday
Bible Reading: 1 Peter 3:7
Word of the Day: Heirs

Peter says that Christian husbands and wives are both heirs of God's grace. An heir is someone who is part of a family and gets all the benefits and rewards of being part of that family. What Peter is saying is that for Christians, God is our Father and he shares with us every good thing. So, when we go to heaven we will live in God's house, eat God's food, and enjoy God's kingdom, which the Bible says even has streets lined with gold.

1. What is an heir? Examples include someone who gets to enjoy everything in their family and has a huge inheritance waiting for them.
2. Who are God's heirs? All Christians.
3. What kind of things do you think God will have for you to enjoy in Heaven?
4. What do you think Heaven will be like?
5. Who do you want to meet in Heaven?
6. What fun thing do you look forward to doing in Heaven?

Saturday
Bible Reading: 1 Peter 3:7
Word of the Day: Prayer

Peter says that husbands who are mean to their wives will not have their prayers answered by God. What this means is that husbands who do not lovingly serve their wives will not be lovingly served by God until they change and stop sinning against their wives. God says this because sometimes people can be really mean to other people and God wants them to stop being mean and so he warns them to be nice and act like friends.

1. What is prayer? Examples include that prayer is talking to God like a friend.
2. When we pray, do we have to get the words perfect or does God know our heart and what we are trying to say? God knows our thoughts and hearts and so our prayer should be sincere but need not be perfect.
3. How often do you pray to God?
4. Is there anything about praying to God that is hard for you?
5. What are God's answers to our prayers? Yes, no, or later on.
6. Why does God sometimes not answer the prayers of people? If they are being mean to other people, God wants them to stop being mean and so he tells them he will answer their prayers and help them only if they want to be nice to people.

WEEK 6: 1 PETER 3:8-22

Sunday
Bible Reading: 1 Peter 3:8–17
Word of the Day: Sympathy

Peter says that Christians are supposed to have sympathy. What this means is that Christians are supposed to be loving and consider other people and their feelings and needs. No one is perfect, everyone sins, and God is working on every Christian all the time. Sympathy is when we are loving, patient, kind, and helpful with one another. Sympathy is understanding that some people are just not good at some things, or that they won't be good at some things until they learn more, which takes time. Sympathy is not demanding that people be perfect but loving them to help them always grow to be more like Jesus.

1. What are some ways that we can act without sympathy? Examples include being mean, impatient, demanding, or expecting everyone to be like us.
2. Who has shown you sympathy? How?
3. Who have you shown sympathy to? How?
4. How does God have sympathy with us? Examples include He is patient with us, serves us, and works hard to help us all the time.
5. When you are with younger children, how is it hard for you to

have sympathy for them?
6. Are there any people it is hard for you to treat with sympathy? Who?

Monday
Bible Reading: 1 Peter 3:8–17
Word of the Day: Brothers

Peter says that Christians should have love for one another like siblings. What he means is that because God is our Father, the church is like a family, and we should treat other Christians kind of like brothers and sisters treat one another. Brothers and sisters love one another, spend time together, do things together, help one another, and sometimes disagree or even fight but always work it out because they love one another. With Jesus, we get our family and spiritual brothers and sisters, in addition to our family so we are blessed twice.

1. How is the church like a family? God is our Father and Christians are like brothers and sisters.
2. How do loving brothers and sisters treat one another?
3. What are some ways that brothers sin against one another?
4. What does the Bible mean when it says Christians should love one another like brothers and sisters do?
5. Is there any Christian who has loved you like a brother or sister? Who?
6. Is there any Christian whom you have loved like a brother or sister? Whom?

Tuesday
Bible Reading: 1 Peter 3:8–17
Word of the Day: Tender heart

Peter says that God the Holy Spirit helps us to have a tender heart. A tender heart is a heart that loves God, loves people, feels bad when someone has been hurt or sinned against, and wants to do the right thing. The opposite of a tender heart is a hard heart that does not submit to God, treat people nicely, or apologize when something wrong is done. Everyone gets a hard heart sometimes and needs to pray to Jesus, asking him to help us have a tender heart.

1. What is a tender heart?
2. What is the opposite of a tender heart? A hard heart.

3. How is a tender heart different than a hard heart?
4. Are people with tender hearts loving and happy? Why?
5. How is your heart lately – more tender or hard? Why?
6. When you think of someone with a tender heart that you know, who comes to mind?

Wednesday
Bible Reading: 1 Peter 3:8–17
Word of the Day: Defense

In sports, there is usually offense and defense. Defense is how we keep our opponents from scoring more points on us and protecting our team. Sometimes, people have questions about Christianity that we need to give answers for so that we are defending our faith. Peter says that Christians should lovingly answer any questions non-Christians have about Jesus, the Bible, and Christianity. This is called defense.

1. Are there any people who have asked you questions about the Bible or Jesus or Christianity? Who asked and what questions did they ask?
2. Are there any questions you have about Jesus or the Bible or Christianity that we could help answer?
3. Why is it better to try and answer people's questions rather than argue and fight with them if they are being mean to you for being a Christian?
4. Parents, this is a good time for you to share the big questions you have wrestled with and how God helped you through books, friends, sermons, etc., to get the answers you needed.

Thursday
Bible Reading: 1 Peter 3:18–22
Word of the Day: Noah

Peter uses Noah as an example for us to learn from. Noah lived in the desert when God told him to build a huge boat called an ark. Hebrews 11:7 says that Noah had faith in God. Noah demonstrated this faith by building an ark in the middle of the desert with the help of his sons for about 120 years. The ark was an enormous 1.4 million cubic feet, or the size of 522 modern railroad boxcars and was shaped like a battleship. People made fun of Noah even though he preached for them to have faith in God. The flood eventually came, and everyone but Noah and his family died because no one else got on the ark to be saved. Like Noah, today we live by faith that one day Jesus will come back and everyone will be sent to heaven or hell. Until that day comes, people will make fun of Christians like they made fun of Noah. We should still love people and preach the gospel to them like Noah did in hopes that they will have faith in God and will not suffer in hell like the people suffered in the flood.

1. Tell me/us the story of Noah as best you can in your own words.
2. What did Noah do that showed he had faith in God? He spent 120 years building the ark.
3. What did people think of Noah while he was building he ark? They made fun of him.
4. Did Noah stop building the ark so that people would stop making fun of him? No.
5. Should we stop doing what is right because people make fun of us? No.
6. Will Jesus rescue us forever like He did Noah and his family? Yes.
7. Noah and his whole family loved and served God together. Why do you think it is important that our family love and serve God together?

Friday
Bible Reading: 1 Peter 3:18–22
Word of the Day: Baptism

Peter says that Jesus died, was buried, and rose from death to cleanse us from our sins. He also says that Christians show that they belong to Jesus by being baptized. In baptism, we are put under the water like Jesus was put under the earth, and then brought up like Jesus rose from death. In doing this we show that we believe in and belong to Jesus and that he cleanses us from sin like water cleanses us from dirt.

1. How does baptism remind us of Jesus?
2. Does baptism make you a Christian? No, believing in Jesus makes you a Christian but Christians who believe in Jesus get baptized to show they believe.
3. Have you ever seen someone get baptized? What did you think?
4. How does Jesus cleanse us from sin like water cleanses us from

dirt?

5. Have you been baptized? If so, what was it like? If not, are you a Christian and would you like to be? Parents, this is a good time for you to see if your children are truly regenerated Christians and whether they are ready to be baptized. It is also a good opportunity to share with your kids how you became a Christian, and what your baptism was like. If you've not been baptized, maybe you can be baptized with your child.

Saturday
Bible Reading: 1 Peter 3:18–22
Word of the Day: Angels

Peter says that Jesus rules over all the angels. Unlike God, angels were created. Unlike God, an angel does not know everything, cannot do anything because they are not as powerful as God, and cannot be everywhere at one time. Angels are good spirits who love God, worship God, and serve God by helping God's people. Unlike people, angels do not have a body and they never die.

1. What is an angel?
2. Are angels as powerful as God?
3. Who made angels?
4. How do angels serve God?
5. Do angels have bodies like people do?
6. What do you think it will be like to meet angels in Heaven?
7. What questions do you have about angels?

WEEK 7: 1 PETER 4:1-11

Sunday
Bible Reading: 1 Peter 4:1–11
Word of the Day: God's will

Peter says that Christians should live their lives according to God's will for them. This means that we cannot always do what other people tell us, or even what we want to do. Instead, we are to trust that God is smarter than we are, loves us, and that doing what he says is always best.

1. Why is it best to do God's will for our lives?
2. How does reading and studying the Bible help us know God's

will?

3. How does prayer help us know God's will?

4. How do Christian family and friends help us know God's will?

5. In what other ways can we learn of God's will for our lives?

Monday
Bible Reading: 1 Peter 4:1–11
Word of the Day: Idolatry

Peter says that sin is ultimately caused by idolatry. Idolatry is when we love something or someone more than God. Sometimes, idolatry is taking good things (like sports, video games, school, or friends) and making them more important to us than God so that they become bad things because we are not using them rightly.

1. What is idolatry?
2. Which people and their opinions of you could become more important to you than God?
3. Which things do you enjoy so much that they could become more important to you than God?
4. How is Jesus better than idols? Examples include He loves us, serves us, and lets us enjoy the good things he gives without worshiping them.

Tuesday
Bible Reading: 1 Peter 4:1–11
Word of the Day: Hospitality

Hospitality is opening our life and home to welcome people in and build friendships with them. Hospitality begins with God who has become our friend and welcomes us into his home for a huge party in heaven (Isa. 25:6–8). Hospitality includes having friends and family over, and especially neighbors and non-Christian friends. People do not often have others over to their homes for dinners and parties anymore, so this is an important ministry for Christians to love people.

1. What is hospitality?
2. What are some fun times you have had eating and playing at other people's homes?
3. What are your happiest memories of having people over to eat and play at your home?
4. When you have people over, what can you do to be unselfish

and serve them?

5. Which people should you invite over to your home? Parents, you may want to start planning more hospitality (if you don't do much at present) by hosting a small group for your church, scheduling play dates, or having the neighbors over for a social time or holiday party.

Wednesday
Bible Reading: 1 Peter 4:1–11
Word of the Day: Grumbling

Peter says that a common sin for people is grumbling. Grumbling is when we talk back, argue, complain, and generally just have a bad attitude. The best-known grumblers in the Bible were the Israelites in the Old Testament. God made them walk around the wilderness for 40 years because they would not stop grumbling against their leader, Moses, and God himself. They grumbled about everything from the food God gave them to eat to the water he gave them to drink.

1. What is grumbling?
2. Is grumbling a sin?
3. How long did the Israelites grumble in the days of Moses?
4. When was the last time you grumbled?
5. What do you grumble about most often?
6. Does grumbling help anything or make anything better?

Thursday
Bible Reading: 1 Peter 4:1–11
Word of the Day: Spiritual gifts

Peter says that rather than grumbling about what we don't like, Christians should try and make the world a better place by using their spiritual gift(s) to serve people and make things better. Every Christian has at least one spiritual gift, and some Christians have more than one. Spiritual gifts are abilities God gives us to do ministry. When we use our spiritual gift(s) we are often happy because we are doing what God made us to do. Some of the spiritual gifts are teaching, leading, evangelism, helping, mercy, service, Biblical counseling, encouragement, wisdom, administration, giving, faith, discernment, and hospitality.

1. What is a spiritual gift?

2. Who has spiritual gifts?
3. What kinds of things do you like to do for other people?
4. What kinds of things are you good at?
5. What might your spiritual gift be?
6. Why is helping people better than grumbling about them and more like how Jesus treats us?
7. Who has been a blessing to you by using their gifts to help you?

Friday
Bible Reading: 1 Peter 4:1–11
Word of the Day: Ministry

Peter teaches that every Christian, no matter how young they are, has important ministry to do. In this way, every Christian is a bit like a pastor who loves and helps people. Peter teaches that our ministry is with our hands and our mouths. With our hands we serve people for Jesus, and with our mouths we speak to people about Jesus.

1. What is ministry?
2. Who is in ministry?
3. What are the two kinds of ministry?
4. Do you feel you are better at helping people with the works of your hands or the words of your mouth?
5. Why is it nice of God to let us each do ministry?
6. Who has ministered to you?
7. Who can you minister to this week?

Saturday
Bible Reading: 1 Peter 4:1–11
Word of the Day: Glory

Peter says that all glory belongs to Jesus. He means that Jesus should be the most important person in our life and that we should do everything we can to make sure that other people see how wonderful He is. The word glory means something like the blazing glow that happens in a fire. When we sit around a fire and put a stick in, the end of that stick glows red from therefore, or glories. So, when we walk with Jesus and stay close to him, we too burn with the glory of God so that other people see how Jesus changes our life and he gets all the glory for the good things we have and do.

1. Who should get all the glory?

2. How is glorying in Jesus sort of like putting a stick in a fire?
3. Do angels glorify Jesus? Yes, they serve him and sing songs of worship to him.
4. How does our singing worship songs to Jesus glorify Him?
5. Is it possible to glorify Jesus in every area of life?
6. Is there any area of your life in which you are struggling to glorify Jesus?

WEEK 8: 1 PETER 4:12-19

Sunday
Bible Reading: 1 Peter 4:12–19
Word of the Day: Rejoice
Peter says that even though life can be very difficult, we need to find reasons to rejoice in God. God is good, and He is always good to us. Yet, when life is hard it can be difficult to see the ways God is being good to us. So, we should work even harder in tough times to see God's grace and love in our lives. One day when Jesus returns, and sin is gone, there will be nothing but rejoicing forever.

1. Why should we rejoice in God?
2. Why is rejoicing in God sometimes harder when life is tough?
3. What reasons do you have to rejoice in God?
4. What has God done in your life that you should be thankful for?
5. Who is the most joyful person you know?

Monday
Bible Reading: 1 Peter 4:12–19
Word of the Day: Spirit
Peter says that Christians can worship God because they have the Holy Spirit. The Holy Spirit is God and the third member of the Trinity. He has forever lived in relationship with God the Father and God the Son (Jesus Christ) in perfect love, communication, and joy kind of like a perfect family. Because the Holy Spirit lives in Christians, he teaches us about God, convicts us of sin that separates us from God, and enables us to worship God. The Holy Spirit lives in Jesus and also helped Him, so the Holy Spirit knows how to help us become like Jesus.

1. Who is the Holy Spirit?

2. How does the Bible teach us that the Holy Spirit is a person and not just a force? He is a person who can be grieved (Eph. 4:30), resisted (Acts 7:51), and insulted (Heb. 10:29).
3. Is the Holy Spirit God? Yes (Acts 5:3–4; 2 Cor. 3:17–18).
4. Does the Holy Spirit live in everyone? No, only Christians (Eph. 1:13–14).
5. How did the Holy Spirit help Jesus when Jesus was your age?
6. What does the Holy Spirit do for Christians? Examples include He saves us, convicts us of sin, teaches us the Bible He inspired to be written, gives us spiritual gifts, gives us love for Jesus, helps us to pray, and helps us to worship God.

Tuesday
Bible Reading: 1 Peter 4:12–19
Word of the Day: Worship

Everyone worships someone or something. Worship is giving ourselves for someone or something because they are most important to us. Worship includes singing but is much bigger than that and is our whole life. Worship is who or what is most important to you. Some people worship their job, or their hobby, or their sport, or what other people think of them. Christians worship God the Father through God the Son by the power of God the Holy Spirit. Peter says that when people are being made fun of for being Christians it is a good time to worship God by staying devoted to Him and doing what is right.

1. What is worship?
2. What is the opposite of worship? Idolatry, worshiping someone or something other than God.
3. Is worship just singing or is it singing plus all of life?
4. Why do some people stop worshiping God when people make fun of them for being a Christian?
5. Do you worship God? Why or why not?
6. Is there anything we could do to include more worship singing in our family? Parents, this may include buying some worshipful music for your child, listening to worship music in the car and singing together, etc.

Wednesday
Bible Reading: 1 Peter 4:12–19

Word of the Day: Consequence

When we sin and do a bad thing, there are consequences. For example, when we are mean, people don't want to be our friend. When we are selfish, other people don't get to enjoy the things we have. When we do something wrong, we also feel bad. When we sin and do bad things, everyone is hurt, including God, other people, and ourselves. When we learn from our mistakes and see how we hurt people, it helps us not do the bad things anymore but change.

1. What is a consequence?
2. What are the consequences of sinful choices for us and other people?
3. Who has sinned against you, doing a bad thing, and making you suffer?
4. Who have you sinned against, doing a bad thing, and making them suffer?
5. Who do you know that used to be a sinful person doing bad things that caused problems in their life but has changed and doesn't do those things anymore? Parents, this is a good opportunity to share with your kids in an appropriate way sinful mistakes you have made in your life, the consequences, and how God has helped you.

Thursday

Bible Reading: 1 Peter 4:12–19

Word of the Day: Shame

Peter says that people who sin and do not repent and change feel shame. This means that they feel guilty, bad, sad, and frustrated. People who have shame tend to hide what they did from other people and often try to pretend that things are fine when they are not. However, Peter says that Christians should not be stuck in feeling ashamed. This is because Jesus died to forgive our sins, take our shame, and sends the Holy Spirit to help us to feel forgiven, change, and not keep doing the things that are wrong.

1. Why do people feel shame?
2. What is shame?
3. What kinds of things do ashamed people often do?
4. How should Christians deal with shame from sin?
5. Is there any secret sin you are ashamed of?

Friday
Bible Reading: 1 Peter 4:12–19
Word of the Day: Trust

Peter says that when our life is difficult, and people are making fun of us for being a Christian, it is more important than ever to trust God. This includes trusting that He does exist, does love us, will help us, is ultimately in control of our lives, and will sort everything out and make it right. This trusting in God is one of the ways that we worship God.

1. What does it mean to trust God?
2. Why is it sometimes harder to trust God in tough times?
3. Have you ever struggled to trust God? Explain.
4. Parents, take some time to explain to your children a season or circumstance in which you struggled to trust God, what you learned through that struggle, and answer any questions they may have about your experience in trusting God.

Saturday
Bible Reading: 1 Peter 4:12–19
Word of the Day: Good works

Peter says that even when life is tough and people are making fun of us for being Christians, we still need to do good works. Good works are those things we do because God loves us, and we want to obey him because we love him. Good works is simply doing the right thing even when no one sees us except God and even when people are not thankful for what we do. We do good works because we love God and people, and we want to help people know God.

1. What are good works?
2. What good works did Jesus do even when life was difficult?
3. Why should a Christian do good works?
4. What kind of good works does God want you to do? Do chores, help a younger sibling, finish my homework, etc.
5. What things make it hard for you to keep doing your good works?
6. Who has done some really good things to help you?

WEEK 9: 1 PETER 5:1-14

Sunday
Bible Reading: 1 Peter 5:1–5
Word of the Day: Witness

Peter says that he was a witness to the sufferings of Jesus Christ. This means that he knew Jesus personally and was with him for three years. Peter saw Jesus get arrested, crucified, and rise from death. In a day when there were no video cameras or audio recorders, the testimony of an eyewitness was the best way to know the facts about someone's life. So, Peter is one of the best people to tell us the truth about Jesus.

1. What was Jesus' relationship with Peter?
2. How many years was Peter a disciple of Jesus?
3. Was there anyone who saw more of Jesus' three years of ministry than Peter? No, Peter saw Jesus the most.
4. If people disagree with Peter about Jesus' life, should we believe Peter or them?
5. How do we know Peter is not lying about Jesus? He suffered for being a Christian and was crucified upside down, which is not something he would have endured for a lie.
6. Who knows you the best and has been a witness in your life like Peter was a witness in Jesus life?

Monday
Bible Reading: 1 Peter 5:1–5
Word of the Day: Leader

Peter says that leaders are to be loving, generous, patient, and set an example for people. Everyone has leaders in their life. When you are little, you have parents, coaches, teachers, and ministry leaders. When you are older, you have bosses at work, pastors at church, and the government. It is important for people who are leaders to lead like Jesus. And, it is important for people to also respect and follow their leaders.

1. Why does God give some people the authority to lead other people?
2. What should you do if someone in authority (e.g., parent, pastor,

teacher, coach) tells you to do something that is a sin?
3. What should you do if someone in authority asks you to do something that is in the Bible?
4. What happens to people, including children, who do not obey godly authority?
5. Since Satan was proud, and Jesus was humble, why is it so important to be humble and not proud?
6. Who is a person you know that is humble?
7. Who is a good example of a godly leader that you know?

Tuesday
Bible Reading: 1 Peter 5:1–5
Word of the Day: Young people

Peter says that sometimes young people have a hard time listening to and obeying older people. For children, this includes parents, grandparents, and teachers. Still, younger people need to learn to listen to and obey older people who love them and love Jesus. This is so that the older people can help teach and train the younger people.

1. Why do young people sometimes not listen to older people?
2. Which older people in your life are you supposed to listen to?
3. Are there any things that older people tell you to do that you do not feel is right?
4. Why should you be thankful that there are older people in your life to love you and help you grow up?
5. What happens to kids who don't listen to older people?
6. Which younger person do you know that does a good job listening to older people who help them learn and grow?

Wednesday
Bible Reading: 1 Peter 5:6–14
Word of the Day: Anxiety

Anxiety is anything that makes us worried, stressed out, and frustrated. Everyone has anxiety in their life at various times for various reasons. Peter tells us the best thing to do when we are anxious is to cast our anxieties on God because He cares for us.

1. What is anxiety?
2. Does God care for us? Explain.
3. Since God cares for us, how can we cast our anxieties on Him

like handing something too heavy for us to carry to someone stronger to carry for us?

4. What can you do to turn to God when you have anxiety (e.g. pray, get some alone time to journal or think, read the Bible, sing worship songs to God)?

5. It there anyone or anything in your life that you are anxious about lately?

Thursday
Bible Reading: 1 Peter 5:6–14
Word of the Day: The devil

Peter says that the devil is like a lion roaming around looking for people to hurt. The devil is a bad angel who does not love God, does not tell the truth, and wants us to sin and disobey God. Peter tells us to resist him, which means we are to love God, believe the truth of the Bible, do what God wants us to do, and ask God to help us and forgive us when we sin.

1. Who is the devil?
2. As you look at how people treat each other in the world, how do you think the devil is behind so many bad things?
3. What kinds of things does the devil want us to do?
4. How can we resist the devil?
5. Is Jesus more powerful than the devil? Parents, this is a good time to share some ways that the devil has worked in your life, but that Jesus has proven more powerful and helped you.

Friday
Bible Reading: 1 Peter 5:6–14
Word of the Day: Amen

As he nears the end of his letter, Peter says "amen" a word which means "let it be" or "yes, I agree". When people say "amen," they are agreeing with God and saying with their mouth that what God says is good. Nearly every time "amen" is used in the Bible, it is spoken by worshipers who agree with a portion of Scripture that has been taught or read, or a word that has come from God. So, it is okay when we hear a sermon in church or hear someone teach the truth of the Bible to say "amen" out loud to show that we agree with it.

1. What does "amen" mean?

2. Why is it a good thing for us to sometimes say "amen"?
3. Why is it good for us to close our prayers with "amen"?
4. Are there any parts of the Bible or worship songs you like so much that when you hear them you want to say or shout "amen"? Which ones?

Saturday
Bible Reading: 1 Peter 5:6–14
Word of the Day: Friends

Peter tells the Christians that they should greet one another with a holy kiss. In that day, that was how people who were friends said hello to one another. In our day, some people still greet one another with a kiss, like a husband and wife, or a parent or grandparent who gives a kiss to their children or grandchildren. But most of the time shaking hands or hugging is how we say hello and only a parent or grandparent should give a kiss on the head or cheek to a child. The big idea Peter is teaching is that Christians are to be friends with one another and greet one another in love.

1. Who are some of your best friends?
2. Should we kiss people we meet? No, only our parents or grandparents.
3. What are some nice ways to greet people, especially our friends?
4. Who are your friends?
5. How does it make you feel when your friends greet you lovingly?
6. What can you do to be nicer and kinder to your friends?

NOTES

1. Paul J. Achtemeier, Harper & Row and Society of Biblical Literature, Harper's Bible Dictionary (San Francisco: Harper & Row, 1985), 776.]
2. G.R. Osborne, "Peter, the Apostle," ed. J.D. Douglas and Philip W. Comfort, Who's Who in Christian History (Wheaton, IL: Tyndale House, 1992), 549.
3. Michael Green, The Message of Matthew: The Kingdom of Heaven, The Bible Speaks Today (Leicester, England; Downers Grove, IL: InterVarsity Press, 2001), 179–180.
4. Doug Redford, The Life and Ministry of Jesus: The Gospels, vol. 1, Standard Reference Library: New Testament (Cincinnati, OH: Standard Pub., 2007), 183.
5. A. F. Walls, "Peter," ed. D. R. W. Wood et al., New Bible Dictionary (Leicester, England; Downers Grove, IL: InterVarsity Press, 1996), 907.
6. Karen H. Jobes, 1 Peter (Grand Rapids: Baker, 2005), 8.
7. David H. Wheaton, "1 Peter," in New Bible Commentary: 21st Century Edition, 4th ed., ed. D. A. Carson et al. (Leicester, England; Downers Grove, IL: Inter-Varsity Press, 1994), 1369.
8. F. F. Bruce, New International Bible Commentary (Grand Rapids, MI: Zondervan Publishing House, 1979), 1550.
9. D. A. Carson, New Testament Commentary Survey (Grand Rapids: Baker, 1986/2007), 136.
10. Peter Achtemeier, 1 Peter (Minneapolis: Fortress, 1996), 35–36.
11. Karen H. Jobes, 1 Peter (Grand Rapids: Baker, 2005), 19.
12. Karen H. Jobes, 1 Peter (Grand Rapids: Baker, 2005), 22–23.
13. Against Heresies, 36.; Ecclesiastical History, 2.25.8; 2.15.2; 3.1.2–3.
14, Walter A. Elwell and Barry J. Beitzel, "Caesars, The," Baker Encyclopedia of the Bible (Grand Rapids, MI: Baker Book House, 1988), 396.
15. Karen H. Jobes, 1 Peter (Grand Rapids: Baker, 2005), 9.
16. Peter Achtemeier, 1 Peter (Minneapolis: Fortress, 1996), 35–36.

MARK DRISCOLL

With Pastor Mark, it's all about Jesus! Mark and his wife Grace have been married and doing ministry together for over twenty-five years. They also planted The Trinity Church with their five kids in Scottsdale, Arizona as a family ministry (thetrinitychurch.com) and started Real Faith, a ministry alongside their daughter Ashley that contains a mountain of Bible teaching from Pastor Mark as well as content for women, men, pastors, leaders, Spanish-speakers, and more.

Mark has been named by Preaching Magazine one of the twenty-five most influential pastors of the past twenty-five years. He has a bachelor's degree in speech communication from the Edward R. Murrow College of Communication at Washington State University as well as a master's degree in exegetical theology from Western Seminary in Portland, Oregon. For free sermons, answers to questions, Bible teaching, and more, visit **RealFaith.com** or download the **Real Faith app**.

Together, Mark and Grace have authored "Win Your War" and "Real Marriage". Pastor Mark has authored numerous other books including "Spirit-Filled Jesus", "Who Do You Think You Are?", "Vintage Jesus", and "Doctrine".